Sola Fide
& Merit

The Catholic Perspective on Paul
& the Dialectic of Salvation

T.D. Barrett

IHP OECUMENICUM

Originally published January 2025. Revised edition, August 2025.

IHP OECUMENICUM
An Imprint of Illative House Press, LLC
500 E. Elm St.
West Frankfort, IL 62896
IllativeHousePress.com

All IHP publications are available through Amazon.com.

Hardcover ISBN: 979-8-9915912-8-7
Paperback ISBN: 979-8-9915912-7-0
E-book ISBN: 979-8-9915912-9-4

Cover artwork: Rembrandt, public domain, via Wikimedia Commons
Cover design: Illative House Press

Disclaimer: Unless otherwise noted by the author, all Scripture quotations and quotations of historical sources presented in this work are based on the author's own translation and sourcing. IHP makes no warranty regarding the accuracy of these translations or sources.

**ILLATIVE
HOUSE**

PRESS

Table of Contents

Introduction

I was not always Christian. In fact, for the majority of the first 20 years of my life, I was an atheist. And my experience meeting the Lord, when I did meet Him, was one of profound grace. I had lived a life of selfishness and self-destructive behavior, taking for granted and taking advantage of those who loved me. Then, one day, amid my sins, the Lord infused into me a desire for Himself and, in the darkness of my situation, revealed Himself to me. Within the course of a few short weeks, my entire pattern of life changed. Whereas before, I took pride in things that were sin, I now found myself driving the speed limit with my seat belt on, listening to Jamie Grace on Christian radio, singing along with a smile on my face, just rejoicing to know how much God loves me. A few months later, I became interested in theology and found myself listening to debates about the relationship between faith and works in our salvation. Now, my own experience of being saved and transformed through faith, despite never having done good in my life, was powerful support for the Protestant view on the subject. I would find myself regularly debating Catholics about it: I had been saved, born again, radically and supernaturally transformed and made holy when I came to believe in Jesus, and not because I had done any good works. What Catholics didn't understand, I thought, was that a transformed life and the good works that flow from it are the product of being born-again and saved and not the cause of it. Over the course of the next couple of years, I developed a passion for ministry and entered seminary. However, along the way I noticed that some believers were not living how Scripture says we need to. I struggled to make sense of this (doesn't faith automatically produce works?) but remained convinced that the Protestant view was correct, and that Catholics were just misguided "religious" people who didn't understand how conversion, faith, and works work together.

My frustration and confusion remained until one morning when I sat down and read the Book of Acts and the Book of Romans in one sitting. My eyes were opened as I realized that St. Paul's[1] arguments about the "works of the law" in Romans were arguments he made in the context of his struggles

---

[1] The following naming convention is used throughout with reference to the designation Saint or St.: the first time the person is mentioned (aside from headings), the designation is used. Thereafter, common usage of the person's first or last name is used unless included in a direct quote that presents the person differently. The same convention is applied with key Protestant figures.

with the Judaizers and Jewish hostility towards Gentiles. Paul was talking about Gentile inclusion and the Mosaic law! Previously, I had understood his doctrine of justification purely in terms of good works and earning salvation ("circumcision" being just a synecdoche for "religion"), completely overlooking the historical context. In my excitement, I thought I was the first to discover his true meaning. I was disappointed when I learned that James Dunn had beaten me to it by a few decades. I then discovered the "New Perspective on Paul" and was a zealous advocate for it for the next few years.

During those years, I became convinced of Catholicism but increasingly wrestled with certain aspects of Catholic spirituality, and ultimately reverted to a desire for Protestantism and would spend two years trying to prove the Catholic faith wrong. In my continued study of justification, I eventually saw that the New Perspective didn't do full justice to Paul's arguments about faith and works. While Paul was definitely talking about Gentile inclusion and the Mosaic law, he also, at times, seemed to contrast faith and works generally. His rejection of boasting seemed targeted not just at ethnic privilege but also at self-righteousness. Upon discovering the work of St. Augustine, I discovered that I was not the only Catholic who perceived these issues in Paul. Before long, I found that many Catholic saints (even doctors of the Church) had read Paul this way: *sola fide* - at least as far as faith and works in Paul goes - had a long Catholic history and was not a Protestant innovation. After a couple of years of trying to prove to myself that I could be Protestant, I ultimately conceded that I had no actual argument. I could find no errors in Catholic dogma, and my experience of grace in the Sacraments had been undeniable. My studies showed me that I could understand Paul in terms of *sola fide* while being faithful to the Catholic tradition - but as of yet, I still was not sure how to make sense of the seeming contradiction between the varied biblical and catholic teachings on *sola fide*, works, merit, etc. I could not conceive of how these diverse teachings fit together until a conversation I had with a fellow student...

I want to begin by saying thanks to that student, the brother (now father) Chrysostom Mijinke, O.P. It was one day after a class on the Pauline literature that he mentioned to me in passing that the question of salvation seemed to him to consist in a "dialectic" between grace and works. The moment I heard him say that word - dialectic - a light turned on in my head, and I have ever since believed that the concept of dialectic is key to understanding the varied biblical teachings on this subject. So, I thank God for the good brother (now father), and much of the inspiration for this book is due to that brief remark and that single word spoken to me years ago. I also want to thank my professors and dialogue partners over the years. The constant aid of fellow Christians pushing back, educating me, sharing their experiences, and serving as a sounding board for my ideas has been invaluable. Thank you also to the good sister Emily, who allowed herself to be used by God to speak truth to me at a time when I needed to hear it most. An infinite thank you to my parents, who have supported me for so long, even in my worst moments. And to my wife, whom I love: Thank you for accompanying me during the writing process and believing in me.

At the beginning of this book, I will briefly sketch out the history of the Lutheran Reformation and the New Perspective on Paul as this provides the background for the dive into the history of Catholic exegesis that follows. The goal is to show, contra those who claim that the 'New Perspective' is Catholic, that the most authoritative Catholic thinkers have understood Paul in an essentially Old Perspective manner, including a particular catholic form of *sola fide*. I then offer a brief excursus in defense of the Old Perspective before moving on to a chapter devoted to everything else the Bible says about salvation. Following that, I proceed to the dialectic of salvation: *sola fide* and merit: salvation is both "by faith alone" and also by works and merit. Ultimately, I agree that *sola fide* should be given pride of place over the other biblical descriptions of salvation (like works/merit) as long as we do not reject the orthodoxy of the other descriptions. The final chapter, a second excursus on the Protestant doctrine of Imputation, could only have been produced due to my many conversations over the years with Lutherans. I am grateful for their feedback there, and I hope my efforts prove illuminating as to just how far we agree and also as to where the Protestant doctrine falls short.

This book is the product of a decade of wrestling, studying in seminaries in both Catholic and Protestant settings and devouring everything I could find. I have attempted to make it (mostly) accessible to lay people and to the uninformed, but I have also tried to make it engaging for the learned, such that scholars on all sides of the aisle, even (perhaps especially) those whose expertise lay in this field, will find arguments challenging their presuppositions. Due to the availability of free texts online, many of the quotes shared in this book are identified merely by reference to where they can be found rather than with a precise footnote citation. I provide footnotes for those texts that cannot be found for free online.

One last note: this book is about tension. This is not an attempt to describe the Gospel in the most clear and fruitful terms possible. In some places, I will give a hint about what I think about that. But this book is about the dialectic inherent within the biblical description itself - the tension between what it says about *sola fide* and what it says about merit. The book is meant to challenge, cut, divide, and ultimately unite back together. But this is not a seamless tapestry; it is two perspectives woven together to form a complementary whole. Not artificially so, but biblically and theologically.

Furthermore, while New Perspective exegesis and specific aspects of Protestant theology are critiqued, popular Catholic preaching is also. Undoubtedly, it is an internal critique: a call for reform rather than an accusation of error. But it is a critique, and the book is driving at correction, demanding we recognize and affirm valid tensions where they exist. There is a time and place for systematizing and smoothing, but systematics are not possible until the tensions of exegesis are laid out plainly. So plainly, we lay them.

> **For we are not seeking victory, but to gain brothers,**
> **by whose separation from us we are torn.**
> (St. Gregory the Theologian)

Chapter 1
The Launch of a Protest

The Justice of God

It was the year 1483, and the discoveries of Columbus and Copernicus would soon transform the world. The Renaissance was in full swing, and in the Catholic Church, centuries of increasing corruption had led to a loss of confidence in traditional authority. Rival claimants to the Papacy, priests with concubines, corrupt bishops using clerical offices for money and power… into this foment, a German bluster of a man named Martin Luther was born. His father had put him on a path to become a lawyer for the family business, but one day, fearing for his life and caught in a lightning storm, that path was altered. Luther cried out to St. Anne, mother of the virgin Mary, begging her to save him, vowing to become a monk if she would. To the great chagrin of Luther's father and against the advice of everyone who knew him, Luther kept the promise, and in 1505, he entered the Augustinian order. From that point on, his life was caught up in the faith.

Martin entered religious life thinking he would find peace and salvation, but after years of practicing the spiritual disciplines, he failed to find any consolation. The prayers, the fasting, the mortifications, vigils, prayers to Saint… and whatever else he was prescribed… they all failed to bring him comfort. Religious life was not helping; in fact, Luther felt more estranged from God than ever. Even the sacrament of confession, designed most especially to bring peace to the sinner, became something of a torture chamber to the man. Had he remembered every sin? Was he truly sorry? He feared, nay he knew, when the scales of justice were weighed, he would be wanting. No matter how many sins he confessed, no matter how many good works he did, no matter how hard he tried to purify himself - he became only all the more aware of his shortcomings and could not escape the feeling of deep inadequacy and guilt before God.

Perhaps Luther was not cut out for the religious life. Perhaps Luther was scrupulous. Whatever the case, part of his trouble had come, he would later tell us, from a teaching of Scripture in the writings of Paul, that "the Gospel reveals the justice of God" (Rom. 1:17). Justice, in Luther's understanding, meant judgment. Example: a just judge condemns the guilty. For Luther, the Gospel thus revealed not the love of God but God's justice in punishing sinners. The Gospel revealed that the offense of sinful men was so great that it brought about the death of Christ Himself. When Luther looked at a painting of Jesus or at a crucifix, he saw only judgment. The blood of Jesus was on sinners' hands - it was on Luther's hands. Christ's face was perpetually that of stern rebuke. He, who was supposed to be his Savior, was, instead of an advocate, seen to be the one prosecuting him. The Cross was Luther's condemnation.

At least, that is how Luther saw things until one day when he grasped hold of the true meaning of that phrase in Paul, that phrase which had so troubled him, that the Gospel reveals the justice of God. It wasn't, after all, a reference to God's judicial action in punishing the guilty. It referred rather to God's merciful saving action, to God's action of saving sinners through faith in what Christ had done for them and not because of anything they had done or could do for themselves. Luther describes his discovery below:

> I had conceived a burning desire to understand what Paul meant in his Letter to the Romans… "The justice of God is revealed in it." I hated that word, "justice of God," which, by the use and custom of all my teachers, I had been taught to understand as referring to that justice by which God is just and by which he punishes sinners and the unjust.

> But I, blameless monk that I was, felt that before God I was a sinner with an extremely troubled conscience. I couldn't be sure that God was appeased by my satisfaction. I did not love, no, rather I hated the just God who punishes sinners…This was how I was raging with wild and disturbed conscience. I constantly badgered St. Paul about that spot in Romans 1 and anxiously wanted to know what he meant.

> I meditated night and day on those words until at last, by the mercy of God, I paid attention to their context: "The justice of God is revealed in it, as it is written: 'The just person lives by faith.'" I began to understand that in this verse the justice of God is that by which the just person lives by a gift of God, that is by faith. I began to understand that this verse means that the justice of God is revealed through the Gospel, but it is a passive justice, i.e., that by which the merciful God justifies us by faith, as it is written: "The just person lives by faith." All at once I felt that I had been born again and entered into paradise itself through open gates.

This is Luther's retelling of the story, dated 1545, so it is in hindsight. But it reflects his journey, something he experienced during the 1510's as he served as professor of the Bible. He had been appointed a Doctor of Theology by his superior for this very reason. The superior, Father Johanne Staupitz, was a confessor and spiritual advisor to Luther, and was all too familiar with the young priest's struggles to find peace with God. He appointed Luther to teach scripture, confident he would find in the word of God a remedy for his troubled conscience. And in the word of God indeed he found it. He did *not* find it, and this is important for understanding everything that follows, he did *not* find it in the labors of religious life. Those labors only aggravated the problem, leaving him with nothing but malice for God.

Perhaps here we should stop for a moment and attempt an explanation. It is not hard to imagine what caused Luther's problem. Although he was a faithful Catholic, living obediently, receiving the sacraments, fasting and praying, and doing everything else he was supposed to be doing, nevertheless, when he looked within himself, he saw the internal inclinations to sin never left, but seemed even more grievous than before. This experience is actually quite typical. Saints throughout the millennia have testified that the holier they became, the more aware of their own sins they became, and the more grievous they understood those sins to be. Ordinary people can relate to this: whenever we take up a hobby and begin to master it, the more adept we become, the more fine-tuned our perception becomes, and the flaws that before seemed inconsequential, we now see through the lens of a microscope. In the spiritual life this occurs as well. An idle word of gossip may seem a trifle, but the violation against charity is seen to be grievous only when we grow enough in charity to see it clearly. While the Christian who pursues purity does become more pure, and experiences less and less inclinations to sin over time, nevertheless this side of Heaven the inclinations never go away entirely. While Catholics have always understood that these inclinations, because they are unwilled by us, do not make us guilty before God, Luther did not understand this. He felt the inclinations themselves were damnable offenses against God that made him worthy of Hell. It is no wonder why he was unable to find peace.

But the doctrine of justification that Luther found in the writings of Paul, brought with it a feeling of peace, love, and assurance into Luther's heart. Luther was convinced of the way forward. It was not the traditions and prescriptions of the Church which had consoled his troubled conscience, but the text of Scripture. The teachings of the Church had actually seemingly made things worse. His spiritual life was in shambles until he learned that he was saved because of Christ, and not because of his own works. Naturally, then, from that point on, Luther considered Paul's doctrine of justification the crux upon which the Christian life stands or falls - and the traditions of the Church suspect (at least, any tradition not clearly proven from Scripture). But it was not until 1517 and a controversy surrounding the sale of indulgences that he was finally backed into a corner, and rejected the (infallible) authority of the Church outright.

The Launch of a Protest

Martin did not set out to be a Reformer, and certainly didn't intend to split from the Catholic Church. He was an obedient Friar and devout Priest, committed to his vows and to ministering to the people of God. What ultimately led to the Protestant Reformation, however, began with a sale throughout Germany of an indulgence. A little background: an "indulgence" is understood as a grant of the Church to sinners in forgiveness of the temporal debt of sin. In Catholic theology, the eternal consequence of sin (Hell), while certainly of primary concern, is not the only consequence. In addition to Heaven and Hell there is a third place, or, better stated, a place of transition between Earth and Heaven, in which the temporal punishment for sin is exacted and the cleansing necessary to enter Heaven achieved. This is called purgatory, and indulgences are said to free one from its pains. A popular way of explaining temporal debt comes from the life of King David in the Book of 2 Samuel. There we learn that David got another man's wife pregnant, and then to cover up his adultery, sent the husband to the front lines of battle to be killed. The prophet Nathan learned of this from God, and confronted David who fortunately repented. Though God forgave David, there were still two penalties incurred: someone from David's own family would sleep with one of his own wives, and the child he conceived through adultery would die. David's sin was forgiven with regards to its eternal consequence, but there were temporal punishments that remained. In Catholic teaching, if temporal punishments such as these are not satisfied during this life, their debt is exacted in the fires of purgatory. Indulgences are grants of the Church to cover such temporal debt.

It was upon people's fears about the fires of purgatory that sellers of an indulgence preyed, as they went about through Germany in Luther's day, telling all who would listen, that, "as soon as you pay a little bit of money, out of purgatory will spring your deceased honey-bunny."[2] However legitimate the

---

[2] The original jingle isn't quite as fun as my rendition: "As soon as the coin in the coffer rings, the soul from purgatory springs."

theology of indulgences may be, and whatever right the Pope may have to grant them, the manner of their sale in Luther's day was wicked and scandalous. The sellers of the indulgence were stoking people's fear rather than their love. Worst of all, at least according to Luther, people were being told they could purchase their loved one's release from purgatory completely apart from any repentance on their part - and even that their own salvation could be purchased likewise. Compounding the situation, the indulgence was being sold because an archbishop bribed the Pope to get a new seat of power to profit from - the Pope allowing the sale of the indulgence as a means of paying the simoniacal debt incurred by doing so. Luther was not aware of that part of the scandal, but was concerned about the pastoral issues stemming from the way the indulgence was being sold, and wrote a letter to the archbishop early in 1517 seeking his help to stop the abuse:

> I grieve over the wholly false impressions which the people have conceived... that if they have purchased an indulgence they are sure of their salvation; again, that so soon as they cast their contributions into the money-box, souls fly out of purgatory...In addition to this, it is said in the Instruction to the Commissaries...that one of the chief graces of indulgence is that inestimable gift of God by which man is reconciled to God, and all the penalties of purgatory are destroyed. Again, it is said that repentance is not necessary in those who purchase souls [out of purgatory] or buy confessionalia.

Luther warned that if action was not taken to correct the situation, he feared someone might publicly criticize the indulgence. Ironically, a few months later, Luther did just that.

On October 31, so says tradition, Luther nailed the 95 Theses to a Church door in Wittenberg. This wasn't an attempt to spark a revolution, but an invitation for debate among theologians. His primary concern was the negative spiritual effects the indulgence was having on the faithful (money instead of repentance, etc.), but he also brought up questions about the Pope's authority over purgatory, and protested the taking of German money to fund foreign projects in Rome. Thanks to the newly invented printing press, the Theses spread like wildfire. The people of Europe, already stoked by a century of anticlerical sentiment, warmly welcomed and applauded the publication of the Theses, and local civil rulers saw an opportunity to rid themselves of the Pope's influence. Those of a more traditional bent, however, were suspicious that Luther's questioning of Papal authority amounted to heresy. It was these competing forces - (1) reforming sentiment combined with civil interest, and

(2) traditionalist concerns of heresy - that catapulted Luther into fame and infamy. Luther wanted to dispute the theology of indulgences, but that would not be granted. On the one side was revolutionary fervor, on the other inquisitional invective.

Called to Augsburg in 1518 to discuss the situation with Luther on behalf of the Pope, Cardinal Cajetan wasn't interested in indulgences. The discussion he wanted was about papal authority. He gave Luther an ultimatum: submit to the authority of the Pope and recant the Theses, or face the consequences (excommunication, or even death). In the following years Luther would be forced more and more into that corner: either recant his writings or reject the authority of the Church. He would not recant. First he rejected only the authority of the Pope, but it was not long until, at the Diet of Worms in 1521, when, pressured deeper into that corner, he finally denied the authority of Church tradition as well.[3] The Catholic Priest Luther, in the face of a Papal Bull demanding that he recant or be excommunicated, scoffed, threw the paper into a fire, and cemented himself into a position of animosity he would never return from.

Sola Fide

It is often said that the formal cause of the Reformation was the question of authority, and the material cause was the doctrine of justification. It would probably be more accurate to say the material cause was the doctrine of indulgences. But while the controversy over indulgences wasn't explicitly about justification, it isn't difficult to see the connection, and it's probably no coincidence that among all the issues which could have sparked the Reformation, it was this one that so took hold of Luther. His struggle with the question of how he, a sinner, could find mercy from a just God, was intimately

---

[3] Luther and Protestants since have retained some semblance of a doctrine of ecclesial authority, and perhaps are even willing to accept a certain human-made authority for the papal office (at least among Anglicans and Lutherans) - but they specifically rejected the infallibility of these authorities. The Church and its voice is something to consider and take seriously, but because it is thought possible of error, it is rejected wherever it seems to do so. This is perhaps similar to how a child respects the authority of their parent: there is a normal obligation for obedience, but because parents can err, the child is not always obligated. The approach is reasonable, but its orthodoxy depends on whether Christ intended the Church to function vis-a-vis *sola Scriptura* as among Protestants, or whether a more enduring communion with the hierarchy is proper.

related to purgatory. What must a person do to get into Heaven? Should the Christian fear what will come after they die? Questions like these dominated his experience as a young friar, and he found answers in the writing of Paul: "The just shall live by faith" and "man is justified by faith apart from works of the law." On the basis of such texts Luther was convinced that a person is saved by the sheer grace of God, received through faith alone, because of what Christ had done on the Cross, and not because of any good works or merits on their part. This was related to his rejection of indulgences; nay, at the heart of it. Works of penance and satisfaction, the earning of indulgences, etc., could not make a person right with God. Only the grace of faith does that. It was this understanding that emboldened his rejection of the Catholic Church.

Luther had labored for years under the toil of penance, fastings, and good works of various kinds, trying to secure peace with God - but it was not until he personally experienced that Pauline teaching of 'justification by faith' that he finally found relief. At last, through faith alone, Luther felt he was born again.[4] Before this experience he had grown to hate God, laboring under

---

[4] It is interesting to note that although he describes his awakening to the doctrine of faith in the specific language of being born again, he did not thereby come to the conclusion that regeneration comes through faith apart from baptism, as many have since, even though he himself apparently did not feel regenerate, despite being baptized as a youth, until he later experienced that awakening through faith. The complex relation between baptismal regeneration and the evangelical conversion experience (i.e., "being born again") is worth meditation, and at least one Catholic, the preacher to the Pope and Cardinal, Fr. Ranerio Cantalamessa, has argued that we can speak of conversion apart from baptism as a 'baptism of the Spirit': "Almost all our thinking is habitually in terms of abstract concepts. A person becomes a child of God, of course we know from theology, we become a member of the body of Christ, The Holy Spirit comes to live in us, giving us sanctifying grace, the theological virtues, all this we know! But all this taking place beyond the level of our consciousness. We notice nothing of it all, in the sense that we feel no different experience, no emotion. This is what students learn in theology! By the baptism we become a child of God, temple of The Holy Spirit, but it's an act of faith, not emotion. There is a lacuna (deficiency/gap) here. And it is exactly this that the charismatic renewal helps the Church to overcome. There has not always been this gap between experience and concepts - especially in the centuries before the rise of scholastic theology ... And we cannot deny that it is possible to have experiences of grace in this life, not just concepts, that give us a sense of freedom, that open us to new horizons, that impress us profoundly and transform... nothing prevents us from calling this experience 'the Baptism in the Spirit'." (From a talk Fr. Cantalamessa gave, *Theology of the Baptism in the Holy Spirit,* published on the YouTube channel entitled "Awakening the Domestic Church").

asceticism but never feeling forgiven. He viewed God solely as punishing judge, but after, God became to Luther the fount of all sweetness. It is no wonder then, that for Luther, the teaching upon which the Christian faith stands or falls, is that answer to the fundamental question of how a sinner is made right with God - by faith alone. His life as a Christian was miserable apart from this, but now that he understood it, his faith was unshakable. This was the Gospel, the revelation of the justice of God in Christ: that a sinner is justified by grace, through faith in what Christ had done, and not because of any good thing they had done or could do.

Luther's own experience had convinced him of the centrality and importance of justification by faith; and in his eyes the Catholic Church had been derelict in teaching it. Remember how Luther described learning the true meaning of "the justice of God": that *"by the use and custom of all my teachers, I had been taught to understand it as referring to that justice by which God is just and by which he punishes sinners and the unjust."* He said that "all of his teachers" - i.e., Catholics - had taught him that the 'justice of God' was God's justice in punishing sinners. Of course, Catholics had told him that mercy was available when penitents atoned for their sins through good works, fastings, vigils, indulgences, and the like. But in Luther's experience those things never actually attained it. No matter how much good he tried to do, he remained aware of his sins and shortcomings. He could not balance the scales of justice. More importantly, he had learned from the writings of Paul that humans cannot earn their salvation. Luther knew that repentance and good works were necessary, but he understood them as the fruit and evidence of true faith, and not something that needs to be added to faith for salvation. When a person truly believes in Christ and receives justifying grace, they are prompted to do all the good works necessary, not in order to be saved, but because they already are. Catholics had erred, in Luther's view, because they did not understand this distinction and proper relationship between faith and works. Works are not added to faith in order to acquire salvation, rather, faith alone saves and produces good works as its natural fruit.

Luther believed the apostle Paul encountered the same confusion about faith and works in his own day with Jewish people who were insisting that Christians needed to add the "works of the law" to their faith in order to merit salvation. The Papists, as Luther called them, were guilty of the same error that Paul's Jewish opponents had been. Catholics in his day, and Jews in Paul's, both insisting that faith alone is not sufficient, and that works need to be added for salvation. Luther describes this connection between Catholics in his day, and Jews in Paul's, in his *Commentary on Galatians.*

Paul attacked the false apostles. We too were willing to make all kinds of concessions to the papists. But we refuse to have our conscience bound by any work or law, so that by doing this or that we should be righteous, or leaving this or that undone we should be damned. The true Gospel has it that we are justified by faith alone, without the deeds of the Law. The false gospel has it that we are justified by faith, but not without the deeds of the Law. The false apostles preached a conditional gospel. So do the papists. They admit that faith is the foundation of salvation. But they add the conditional clause that faith can save only when it is furnished with good works.

In Luther's eyes when you make salvation depend on works you turn the Gospel into the law, turn it into a curse which condemns rather than a promise which saves. What people need to realize, says Luther, is that the law was not given so that we could justify ourselves by our performance of it. Rather, God gave the law so that when we examine ourselves in light of it, we will see our transgressions and our rebellious nature - we actually desire what is forbidden all the more once we realize it is forbidden - and by it be driven to grace. Seeing our guilt and our inability to save ourselves in light of the law, we should cling to the Savior. Through that faith we will then be justified, receive the Holy Spirit, and be prompted to do all the good works required of us.

It was a failure on the part of Catholics, said Luther, like it was a failure on the part of the Jews, to understand the purpose of the law (it was not given so we could save ourselves, but to convict us of our guilt and drive us to grace) and the relationship of faith and works (faith alone saves, and this produces works). These errors lead people to commit the worst sin imaginable: the idolatry of works-righteousness and trying to earn your salvation:

> Paul is now getting ready for the second argument of his Epistle, to the effect that to seek justification by works of the Law, is to reject the grace of God. There is no sin which Paul and the other apostles detested more than when a person despises the grace of God in Christ Jesus. Still there is no sin more common. That is why Paul can get so angry at the Antichrist, because he snubs Christ, rebuffs the grace of God, and refuses the merit of Christ. What else would you call it but spitting in Christ's face, pushing Christ to the side, usurping Christ's throne, and to say: "I am going to justify you people; I am going to save you." By what means? By masses,

pilgrimages, pardons, merits, etc. For this is Antichrist's doctrine: Faith is no good, unless it is reinforced by works.

No wonder Paul employs such sharp language in his effort to recall the Galatians from the doctrine of the false apostles. He says to them: "Don't you realize what you have done? You have crucified Christ anew because you seek salvation by the Law." True, Christ can no longer be crucified in person, but He is crucified in us when we reject grace, faith, free remission of sins and endeavor to be justified by our own works, or by the works of the Law. The Apostle is incensed at the presumptuousness of any person who thinks he can perform the Law of God to his own salvation.

In Luther's theology, trying to earn your salvation is the human sin par excellence, constituting an arrogant idolatry of self, a denial of our guilt, and a rejection of the grace offered us in Christ. The Papists, by thinking that their "works of the law" - their "*masses, pilgrimages, pardons, and merits*" were needed in addition to faith, and could merit justification from God, had made the same mistake as the Jews did in Paul's day.

Luther's understanding of justification would later become a Protestant slogan: "*sola fide*" which is Latin for "faith alone." In its Protestant context, the slogan carries with it all the connotations about the purpose of the law, the sinfulness of works-righteousness, the implied accusations of Catholic error, the condemnation of attempts at earning salvation, etc., that Luther articulated. And Protestants since then, following Luther, have always found their answer to that fundamental question, "how can I, a sinner, find peace with God?", in the Pauline texts about justification and works of the law: peace with God is found in faith alone, and not in good works of any kind. Thus, the heart of all Protestant preaching and spirituality is a piercing critique of human efforts to earn salvation, of all our self-flattery that we are good people, of all our so-called good works…. The critique that all of these, far from attaining what we seek, are actually sins. They constitute a fundamental denial of grace and are an idolatry of self and our own human goodness. Only the empty-hand of faith, which brings forth no merits or works in its grips, which does not cling to self-righteousness but to the cross of Christ alone, only this empty-hand can receive the gift of justification. The 'obedience of faith' then, to which the Gospel calls us, is not so much the denial of self involved in doing good works, but of humbly admitting that we are guilty sinners who can do none.

Chapter 2
A New Perspective

Introspection

The Protestant tradition, following Luther, has always found its answer to that fundamental question, "how can I, a sinner, find acceptance before a just and holy God?" in the writings of Paul, especially the Book of Romans: *by faith, not works*. But in 1963 the Swiss theologian Krister Stendahl argued Paul wasn't answering that question. Paul was an ancient Jew, and Luther's anxiety about personal salvation was driven by a uniquely "western and medieval introspection" that was alien to the psychology of the apostle. Paul did not suffer from the scrupulosity, the terrors of conscience, and the battle with medieval Catholic teachings on merit and purgatory, that Luther did. Paul did not struggle with how he, a sinner, could find peace with God. Stendahl argued that the apostle's claim in Phil. 3:6, that *"as to the righteousness of the law"* he was *"blameless,"* indicated Paul was actually quite confident in his own performance of the law.[5] As far as Paul's own estimation of his work done for the Lord, he had done more, and suffered greater, than all his contemporaries:

> I have worked much harder, been in prison more frequently, been flogged more severely, and been exposed to death again and again... I have labored and toiled and have often gone without sleep; I have known hunger and thirst and have often

---

[5] A consistent point of New Perspective exegesis is this interpretation of Phil. 3:6, which claims on the basis of this text that justification by works of the law never required sinless performance of the law. This exegesis seems to completely miss the point. Paul argues that justification was always by faith, and never by works of the law - not even during the time of the law, did justification come by works of the law. The fact atonement for sin was provided in the law is irrelevant, given this was not provided "so that people could be justified by the law" (something which, Paul tells us, never occurred, indeed, could never occur). Paul's point in Phil 3:6 is not that he had justification in works of the law, but that so far as righteousness could be attained by the law, he was blameless. In the same way that Job, who was a sinner, could be called a righteous man, so too Paul could be said to have been blameless. Not that Paul had righteousness before God on the basis of his works of the law - this righteousness he considered σκύβαλα. The reason such righteousness avails not before God is precisely because "all have sinned", i.e., the problem is that no one has actually done the law.

gone without food; I have been cold and naked. Besides everything else, I face daily the pressure of my concern for all the churches. (2 Cor. 11:16-33)

Why, then, did Paul reject the "works of the law"? If not because they were a source of salvation anxiety? Stendahl argued the reason was simply because the law was no longer of force. There was no problem with an impossible condition of perfect obedience, no intrinsic human inability that the law was supposed to reveal to drive us to grace. The problem with the Jewish insistence upon "works of the law" wasn't with people failing to recognize their depravity or them trying to earn salvation. The problem was simply that the time for the old law and its works had passed away. The prescriptions of Judaism - circumcision, sabbath, etc. - are not expected of Christians. Paul was not struggling with the question of "faith and works" simpliciter, and wasn't in Romans or elsewhere writing a treatise on how sinners could find peace with God. He was answering salvation-historical questions about what happened to the Mosaic Law now that Christ had come, and about the requirements for Gentiles to be included in the people of God.

According to Stendahl, Luther misread Paul through the lens of his own medieval, introspective conscience. He inappropriately imputed his own struggles with Catholic teachings on to the Pauline text:

> It is most helpful to compare these observations concerning Paul with the great hero of what has been called "Pauline Christianity," i.e., with Martin Luther. In him we find the problem of late medieval piety and theology...The manuals for self-examination among the Irish monks and missionaries became a treasured legacy in wide circles of Western Christianity. The Black Death may have been significant in the development of the climate of faith and life. Penetrating self-examination reached a hitherto unknown intensity. For those who took this practice seriously — and they were more numerous than many Protestants are accustomed to think — the pressure was great. It is as one of those — and for them — that Luther carries out his mission as a great pioneer. It is in response to their question, "How can I find a gracious God?" that Paul's words about a justification in Christ by

faith, and without the works of the Law, appears as the liberating and saving answer.[6]

Although Paul's doctrine of justification may have sounded like a direct answer to Luther's struggle with faith and works, that wasn't what Paul was talking about. Paul was not answering the question of how a sinner could find peace with a holy God. *That* question was Luther's own medieval concern, not Paul's. Justification for Paul wasn't about good works and being worthy of salvation, but about the works of the Mosaic Law - the question of how those works related to Gentile Christians (did Gentiles need to become Jewish and get circumcised to follow the Jewish Messiah?). Stendahl focused on the question of Luther's introspective conscience and how Paul wasn't a victim of such anxieties, but his article was at the beginning of a larger movement among Protestant scholars questioning Luther's interpretation of Paul. A few years later this movement would receive its seminal impetus from a study of second-temple Judaism in the Pauline context.

Second Temple Judaism

There were always those who protested Luther's interpretation of faith and works. Some protested because they were convinced from other things in Scripture, i.e., "Faith Alone is wrong because the Epistle of James and the teachings of our Lord both require good works in addition to faith for salvation." But in this section, we focus on another stream of opposition. This other stream, ever more popular among Protestant scholars today, stems from claims about the nature of second-temple Judaism.[7] It must be said that Luther's reading of Paul depends, at least in part, on the idea that what Paul was confronting in 'works' was a Jewish tendency to try to earn salvation. But was this actually true about the Jewish people? They thought they earned salvation? Scholars of Judaism have long protested this as a slander of the Jewish people, but instead of claiming Christians had misunderstood Paul on this point, they just dismissed the New Testament as inaccurate. As a result, their protests were largely ignored by Christian scholars, that is, until the

---

[6] Krister Stendahl, "The Apostle Paul and the Introspective Conscience of the West" *The Harvard Theological Review* 56, 3 (July 1963), 199-215.
[7] "Second Temple Judaism" refers to the ancient form of Judaism that existed between the construction of the second temple and its destruction, the period of time spanning the few hundred years prior to Christ until a few decades after His death/resurrection. This was Judaism at the time of the New Testament, Judaism as the apostle Paul would have known it.

publication in 1977 of E.P. Sanders *Paul and Palestinian Judaism.* This book not only claimed but provided evidence that the Jewish people didn't think they earned salvation - that they nearly universally understood their election into God's covenant as being due to His grace. Sanders wrote this seminal work in part out of a desire to counter antisemitism in light of the Holocaust, and in part as a refutation of scholars like Rudolph Bultmann, who had characterized Jewish theology as petty, legalistic, and merit-driven:

> Repentance itself became a good work which secured merit and grace in the sight of God. In the end the whole range of man's relation with God came to be thought of in terms of merit, including faith itself. Originally obedient loyalty and hope in God's providential guidance, it came to mean faith in retribution or merit. Thus although it was not reckoned explicitly among good works, but placed alongside them, the concept of meritorious faith began to take shape.[8]

Luther's reading is apparent in this quote from Bultmann: The Jewish people conceived of faith in terms of meritorious good works. According to Bultmann, the ancient Jews essentially taught that salvation was for "good people" - that God was the God of the good people, and only good people who deserved salvation would be saved - and that this Jewish doctrine of merit was what Paul was refuting in his doctrine of justification. To refute such claims Sanders displayed over the course of 600+ pages countless examples of second-temple texts demonstrating a widespread belief among the Jewish people that their election was due to God's grace and mercy. Whenever the Jewish people insisted on judgment according to works, this was always in the context of grace: they did not obey God to be accepted by Him, but *because* they were already accepted (and as a way of maintaining that prior acceptance). This system of religion - election by grace and not by works, with subsequent works of obedience meant not to secure favor but to maintain it - Sanders coined "covenantal nomism."

Up until Sanders published *PPJ* it had been accepted by virtually all Protestant scholars that, although God had repeatedly stressed grace and warned about works-righteousness all through the Old Testament, nevertheless, the Jewish people as a whole did not grasp this. Ritualistic legalism and self-righteousness were pervasive, and it was this that Paul confronted in his doctrine of faith and works. But Sanders said, like Stendahl had, that this was an incorrect reading of Paul. Paul was not concerned with the question of

---

[8] Rudolph Bultmann, *Primitive Christianity* (Edinburgh: R & R Clark, 1962), 71.

sinners being worthy of salvation per se. The Jewish people Paul was correcting had a doctrine of election by grace, not merit by works. There was no problem among the Jews of trying to earn or be worthy of salvation. The Jews weren't doing that, and Paul wasn't arguing against it. In Sanders' view, what Paul was actually emphasizing, was merely that Judaism and its law-works was not Christianity: Paul's exclusion of 'works of the law' was not an exclusion of good works or merit (for his opponents would have agreed with him about that), but was a statement about the outdated nature of Judaism. Christianity is what God has done now, and Judaism is not Christianity.

A New Perspective

Sanders' account of second-temple Judaism has been accepted by many if not most Protestant scholars today, convincing a generation that Judaism was not a religion of works-righteousness, and that the Jewish people maintained a priority of grace and covenant in their theology. The Jews at the time of Paul were not guilty of thinking they earned salvation. But this new assumed datum prompted another question: "If the Jewish people weren't attempting to earn salvation, then what, exactly, was Paul arguing against?" The solution proposed by Sanders was that Paul's only real difference with his Jewish opponents was they didn't accept Christ. Paul's whole critique of "works of the law" was simply this: Judaism is not Christianity. But for Protestant scholars who took Scripture seriously, this explanation didn't work. Sanders had made his case that Judaism wasn't a religion of works-righteousness, but Paul clearly had more beef with his Jewish opponents than the mere fact they didn't accept Christ. In fact, it's fairly clear that most of Paul's opponents *did* accept Christ - it was their insistence upon "works of the law" *in addition to faith in Christ* that was the issue. But if the problem with these "works" was not that they were an attempt to earn salvation, then what was Paul's issue? To this question arrived an answer in the mind of Protestant scholar James Dunn, an answer which would form the basis of a movement called "The New Perspective on Paul." In his own words, Dunn explains:

> Sanders only increased the puzzle. If the Judaism of Paul's day also gave such a place to divine election, atonement and forgiveness, then what was Paul objecting to?... I found (the answer) in the context occasioning Paul's first use of the key term, "works of the law," in Gal. 2.16...The "works of the law" in view were evidently the circumcision which "the false brothers" in effect tried to "compel" Gentile believers to

observe (2.3– 4), and the food laws which Peter and the other Jewish believers tried to "compel" Gentile believers to obey...the "boasting" of the "Jew" in Rom. 2.17– 23 is certainly to be understood as a boasting in covenant privilege over against the less-favoured, or rather passed-over Gentiles… A "boasting" of self-confidence and self-reliance, "boasting" in self-achieved righteousness (which I had previously assumed), is remote from the context… "all who are from the works of the law" (Gal. 3.10) was best taken as a reference to those who insisted on a full-scale covenantal nomism (rather than on earning salvation by works righteousness).[9]

To put Dunn's position in brief: the Jewish teaching that Paul was addressing was not that salvation was earned by good works, but rather, that the works of the Mosaic Law, especially those works that separated Jews from Gentiles (circumcision, Sabbath, and Kosher food laws), were obligatory works for Gentile Christians. In essence, Gentiles needed to become Jews, and observe the Jewish law, in order to properly follow the Jewish Messiah. Otherwise, Gentile Christians would be, in comparison with Jews, second-class citizens in the family of God. This was the false teaching Paul was confronting in his attack on "works of the law": the problem was ethnic privilege and exclusivity, not self-righteousness. The works were the works of the Mosaic law, not good works by which people earned salvation.

Dunn's original text for this interpretation - Galatians 2 - is undeniably focused on Gentile inclusion and the question of Mosaic law. Paul opposed St. Peter in Antioch because he had withdrawn from the Gentiles at mealtimes, sitting only with fellow circumcised Jews. But the Gospel teaches that Gentile Christians are full members of the people of God, and that circumcision and the works of the Mosaic Law were not a requirement for one's acceptance. Cf., Gal. 2:15: *"You and I are Jews by birth, and not sinful gentiles, and yet we know that a person is justified by faith and not by works of the law."* Peter and Paul were not justified because they were Jewish, nor because they observed the Mosaic law, but simply because they placed their faith in Christ. To insist that Gentiles were not full and equal members of the covenant because of their failure to be circumcised and observe the Mosaic law (to essentially become Jewish) was a contradiction of this truth of the Gospel.

---

[9] James Dunn, *The New Perspective on Paul* (Heidelberg: Mohr Siebewck, 2007) 1-15.

Starting with this text in Galatians, the "*sola fide*" of Luther seems an alien imposition indeed. Paul wasn't talking about good works and earning salvation. That is nowhere in the context. Rather, he was talking about Gentile inclusion and whether the Mosaic law and Jewishness had abiding relevance for the Christian community. This exegetical insight became the seed of "the New Perspective on Paul." At its heart, the New Perspective is the claim that the Jewish people were not trying to earn salvation, and thus when Paul excludes "works of the law" from justification, the emphasis is not on "works" but on "the law", as in, works of the Mosaic Law. Dunn's initial claim was the works in question were those aspects of the Mosaic law that functioned as ethnic badges which marked out the Jewish people over against the Gentiles (circumcision, kosher diet, and sabbath observance), but other scholars pushed back, and Dunn ultimately agreed that Paul was after was not just the ethnic badges but the entirety of the Mosaic legislation. According to the New Perspective, Paul excluded the works of the law not because Jews thought they earned salvation by them, but because they were outdated and no longer of force now that Christ had come. To insist on such works was to be ethnically divisive and to contradict the Gospel which brought Jews and Gentiles together as one family.

This interpretive tradition has become the nearly dominant reading among Protestants scholars today, at least among those Protestant scholars not particularly committed a priori to the exegesis of the Reformation. That 'Luther got Paul wrong,' that E.P. Sanders' account of Judaism decisive and irrefutable, is now accepted by many as established. Where Luther saw a critique of boasting in personal merit, what was actually in view was the pride of the Jew in being chosen by God over against the Gentile - and that, by grace and not by works. It was not a matter of self-righteousness, but of ethnic privilege. Where good works had been seen, what was actually in view were the works of Jewish Law that were outdated by the coming of Christ. Where the problem of human inability to perfectly obey the law had existed, was rather the simple fact that the law never promised salvation to begin with. Luther went wrong by reading his own struggles with Catholicism back on to the text of scripture, unfairly supposing that the Jewish people Paul encountered were guilty of the same sort of works-righteousness that Luther accused Catholics of:

> As Krister Stendahl warned twenty years ago, it is deceptively easy to read Paul in the light of Luther's agonized search for relief from a troubled conscience. Since Paul's teaching on justification by faith seems to speak so directly to Luther's subjective wrestlings, it was a natural corollary to see Paul's

opponents in terms of the unreformed Catholicism which opposed Luther, with first century Judaism read through the 'grid' of the early 16th century Catholic system of merit.[10]

So, the New Perspective proponents claim: Luther thought Paul was attacking something like the Catholic doctrine of merit that he himself struggled against, but what was actually going on in Paul's day was an intense debate about the Mosaic Law and the inclusion of the Gentiles. While James Dunn is credited with giving us the New Perspective on Paul, Dunn credits E.P. Sanders as giving us "a new perspective on Second Temple Judaism."[11] For Dunn and for those following him, it was the fact that a theology of grace was widespread in Second-Temple Judaism that convinced them of a need for a new perspective on faith and works in Paul. What was the apostle reacting against? Dunn found his answer in Galatians 2. The issue there was ethnic divisions, Gentile inclusion, and the relevance of the Mosaic Law. With this as the context, Paul's arguments have been understood more in terms of the turn of salvation history and the movement from an ethnocentric Jewish cult to an international people of God. The "boasting" Paul was concerned about was not the boasting of a self-righteous moralist, but the boasting of the Jew over against the Gentile. The problem with works was not that people were trying to earn salvation, nor with a law impossible to fulfill, but with a 'sectarian spirit' which sought to keep Yahweh for the Jews alone.[12] Luther got Paul wrong: Judaism was not medieval Catholicism.

---

[10] Dunn, 91-92.
[11] Dunn, 5.
[12] Dunn, 12-14.

Chapter 3
The Old Perspective: A Catholic *Sola Fide*

The New Perspective Is Catholic?

In the first chapter Paul's doctrine of justification was weaponized by Luther to attack perceived Catholic errors with regards faith and works. The Church says works justify and not faith alone - but Paul says faith alone and not works justifies. This emboldened Luther and the Protestant Reformation. But then came along the New Perspective, and for the past 50 years a growing number of Protestant scholars have been telling us that Luther misread Paul on this very point: the apostle wasn't ruling out works per se, but only works "of the (Mosaic) law." For this reason, Protestants who cherish the Reformation doctrine of *sola fide* rise up against the New Perspective as against a Catholic invasion. They say this 'new perspective' is in fact the old Catholic one, and for Protestants to embrace it constitutes an abandonment of the Reformation and a move back towards Rome. Protestant scholar Thomas Schreiner made this claim about the New Perspective, the Reformation, and Catholicism, in a book he wrote on the doctrine of *sola fide*: *"the Reformers and Catholic interpreters disputed this issue... Roman Catholic interpreters argued that 'works of the law' refers to the ceremonial law, while the Reformers emphasized that it encompasses the entire law."*[13] And many have construed the Reformation debate this way - they say that Catholics, in the mold of the New Perspective, understand "works of the law" to mean only the outdated works of Jewish law.

We hear this time and again: Protestants who embrace the New Perspective are embracing the Catholic perspective. For traditional Protestants this is of course an argument against the New Perspective. But for many Catholics it is seen as an argument against Protestantism (i.e., "Your own scholars are telling you that Luther was wrong"). Catholic apologists, even some Catholic scholars, eager to convert Protestants, are often seen advancing this notion that the "works of the law" in Paul have always been understood by Catholics in terms of only the outdated works of the Mosaic law. This New Perspective-based attack on Luther and *sola fide* is perhaps the second most popular anti-protestant argument made by Catholic apologists today (behind only an appeal to ecclesial authority for the existence of the Bible, and a

---

[13] Thomas R. Schreiner, *Faith Alone: The Doctrine of Justification: What the Reformers Taught and Why It Still Matters* (Grand Rapids: Zondervan, 2015), Chapter 19.

skeptical epistemology regarding our ability to know it is the Bible apart from said authority[14]). As a result, many now believe the New Perspective is, quite simply, the Catholic perspective. See Catholic scholar John Bergsma:

> The debate over what St. Paul means by "works of the law" played a major role in the breakup of Western Christianity in the Reformation. Now the (Dead Sea) Scrolls give us the only examples of this theological phrase outside of Paul, and they refer to ritual observance of the Mosaic Law - confirming how Aquinas and other early interpreters understood St. Paul.[15]

Bergsma repeats this another time in the same book, that St. Thomas Aquinas and other earlier Catholic authorities had always understood Paul's "works" as denoting only the ceremonial and ritual aspects of the Mosaic Law and not the moral law:

> Earlier commentators, like Thomas Aquinas...suggested that the phrase "works of the law" must have a specialized sense, referring not to the moral law generally but to the ceremonial and ritual elements of the Mosaic Law which were no longer practiced in the new covenant.[16]

Claims such as these abound, equating the Catholic perspective with the New Perspective. Given Luther claimed Paul's doctrine was proof of Catholic error, it is obvious why Catholics would assume the correct reading must *not* be Luther's reading. We are not wondering why people would marshal the New Perspective as an argument against Protestantism, or why they would think the Catholic reading would be more in line with it than with Luther's. But as understandable as all that may be, a question remains: is the New Perspective really Catholic?

---

[14] Here unfortunately my fellow Catholics have failed to understand Catholic epistemology. Our ability to know any truth of the faith, whether the inspiration of the Bible, the divine institution of the Church, or anything else, is made possible by faith and reason working together. And there are good reasons, of course, for believing in the Bible (and not solely the fact the Church has told us to).
[15] John Bergsma, *Jesus and the Dead Sea Scrolls: Revealing the Jewish Roots of Christianity.* (New York: The Crown Publishing Group, 2019), 219.
[16] Bergsma, 209.

Getting It Right from the Start

The present chapter will show how the most influential authorities in Catholic history have always, going back to the first century, always embraced a basically 'old perspective' reading of Paul. This should be no surprise given the supposed Augustinian nature of the perspective (it actually predates Augustine), but due to the proliferation of misrepresentations on this point, it is necessary to lay out the evidence and show what the history of Catholic interpretation has been. But before we begin, we need to make a clarifying point about the 'old' and 'new' perspectives. It would be easy to say that while the New Perspective understands Paul in terms of the Mosaic Law and Gentile inclusion, the Old Perspective understands him in terms of good works and earning salvation. But this would be inaccurate. Old Perspective interpreters - Luther, Augustine, etc. - have always known that Paul's doctrine of justification was intended to address the questions about Gentile inclusion and the Mosaic Law. While it is fair to say that Luther was perhaps too quick in making the exegetical leap from first-century Jews insisting on circumcision, to medieval Catholics insisting on merit, he did in fact make that leap. We cite one example, from his *Commentary on Galatians*:

> Their objection to Paul's Gospel is...that it was not enough for the Galatians to believe in Christ, or to be baptized, but that it was needful to circumcise them, and to command them to keep the law of Moses...They accused Paul of designs to abolish the law of God and the Jewish dispensation, contrary to the law of God, contrary to their Jewish heritage...The false gospel has it that we are justified by faith, but not without the deeds of the Law. The false apostles preached a conditional gospel. So do the papists. They admit that faith is the foundation of salvation. But they add the conditional clause that faith can save only when it is furnished with good works.

Luther knew the original issue was Jewish believers insisting that Gentile converts needed to get circumcised and follow the Law of Moses. His accusation was that when Catholics taught that good works were necessary in addition to faith, they were guilty of the same sort of "adding on" to the Gospel that Paul's Jewish opponents were guilty of when they insisted that, in addition to faith in Christ, the Gentiles needed to follow the Law of Moses. New Perspective and Old Perspective interpreters agree about this - that Paul was talking about Gentile inclusion and the Law of Moses. The difference between the two perspectives is whether Paul was *also*, in addition to that issue, *also* talking about good works, earning salvation, and things of that sort.

While many New Perspective advocates agree with the theology of *sola fide*, what they deny is that Paul's doctrine of justification is a valid source for deriving that truth. Take for example this quote from Catholic apologist Jimmy Akin, describing his frustration when he was a Protestant, whenever pastors preached on justification apart from good works on the basis of Paul's discussion about "works of the law":

> I know that when I was a Protestant it bugged the fool out of me that I, like my pastor and like all the Protestant preachers I heard, was trying to draw out of Mosaic Law texts a statement that we are not justified by the eternal moral law without any explanation of how the one can be read out of the other. I knew of course that we aren't put right with God by doing that, but as an aspiring exegete committed to faithfully representing what the text actually says, I could not simply suppress the knowledge that Paul was not talking about the eternal moral law in these texts, and so I felt like crying, "Okay! Sure! We don't get right with God by keeping the eternal moral law, but that just isn't what Paul says in these passages! He's clearly talking about the Mosaic Law, not the eternal moral law! The point is true, but the use of the passages to support it is false!"[17]

This captures the mind of many New Perspective interpreters. They might agree that salvation comes to us apart from good works, but they don't think it's exegetically legitimate to derive it from Paul's discussion about justification. And this is true even in texts when Paul defines "works" without qualification. Take for example this passage in Romans 9:

> Rebekah's children were conceived at the same time by our father Isaac. Yet, before the twins were born or had done anything good or bad—in order that God's purpose in election might stand: not by works but by him who calls—she was told, "The older will serve the younger."

Paul here defines "works" in terms of "anything done, good or bad" (μηδὲ πραξάντων τι ἀγαθὸν ἢ φαῦλον), but the Protestant scholar Dr. Chad Thornhill

---

(a New Perspective advocate) argues this is still only about the Mosaic Law and has nothing to do with works in general:

> Paul's next example contains even more force. He notes that before Jacob and Esau were even born "or had done anything good or evil (so that God's purpose in election would stand, not by works but by his calling)" that God had set Jacob apart (loved) but not Esau (hated) (Rom .9:10-13)...The deeds envisioned in these Jewish texts are Torah deeds...He does not offer a general polemic against "deeds" or "merit," as Paul does not oppose such activity.[18]

Dr. Thornhill is a good Protestant and agrees with *sola fide* in terms of his systematic theology, but he finds fault with those who derive the doctrine from Paul's discussion about faith and works. Paul is only opposing works of the Mosaic Law, and not good works or merit in general (indeed, in Dr. Thornhill's mind, "Paul does not oppose such activity"). This negation - Paul is *not* talking about good works and earning salvation - is what characterizes the New Perspective. Its advocates will make this negative claim even when discussing texts like Romans 9 in which works are defined in terms of "anything good or bad".

Another example of this is found in John Barclay's seminal *Paul and the Gift*. Barclay has been heralded as bringing together the best of the Old and New perspectives, and his work has become an instant classic and must-read of all students of Paul. But look at what he says about Rom. 4:4-5 (*"to the one who works his wages are not a gift but what is earned, but to the one who does not work, but trusts in Him who justifies the ungodly, his faith is credited as righteousness"*):

> There is no reason to think that here, or anywhere else in Romans, Paul targets a Jewish (or any other) presumption that one could "earn" salvation by good works. He neither charges nor assumes that Law-keepers boast in their achievements, in the sense of looking to themselves, rather than to God, as the ground of their salvation.[19]

---

[18] Chadwick A. Thornhill, *The Chosen People: Election, Paul and Second Temple Judaism.* (Downers Grove: IVP, 2015), 163-164.

[19] John M.G. Barclay, *Paul and the Gift* (Grand Rapids: Eerdmans, 2015), Section 15.2.

Barclay insists that not even in Rom. 4:4-5, a text which explicitly and unequivocally contrasts earning a wage with receiving a gift you didn't work for - *that not even here* - did Paul have in mind things like earning salvation, trusting in good works, etc.

Both perspectives on Paul ('old' and 'new') agree that Paul was talking about Jews, Gentiles, and the Mosaic Law. The difference between them is that Old Perspective interpreters believe Paul was also talking about good works, earning salvation, and the like. The New Perspective is defined by its rejection, its negation: Paul was not talking about those things. Paul was only talking about the Mosaic Law.

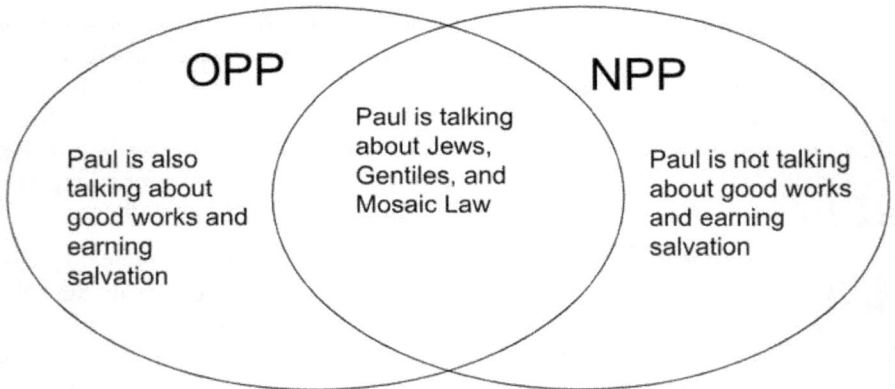

OPP

NPP

Paul is talking about Jews, Gentiles, and Mosaic Law

Paul is also talking about good works and earning salvation

Paul is not talking about good works and earning salvation

This is important for our study because someone who realizes that Paul was talking about the Mosaic Law, Jews and Gentiles, etc., may be quick to embrace the New Perspective. But it would be a hasty error to think the New Perspective is correct simply because Paul was talking about the issue of the Judaizers. The Old Perspective does not deny that Paul was talking about that - in fact many Old Perspective interpreters, in their commentaries on Paul, devote most of their space to discussing the question of the Judaizers, focusing primarily on that issue, and only secondarily/occasionally touching on questions of earning salvation and the like. An Old Perspective interpreter would be happy, in certain contexts - say for example a dispute about the continuing validity of Jewish law - to employ Paul's arguments against the works of the law, without even mentioning those other subjects.

An example from my own life helps illustrate this, for I have a friend who recently became convinced that believers have a continuing obligation to observe the Sabbath, eat Kosher, and generally follow the old law. When I speak to him about this, I rely on Galatians to try to show him his error (i.e., the works of the law are not necessary because the law was only intended to be temporary, cf. Gal. 3:23-25), and I don't have any need - in that context - to bring up the topic of good works and earning salvation.

The writings of St. Jerome demonstrate this same thing. Anyone who begins a study on the New Perspective and the history of exegesis will immediately come across claims that Jerome understood Paul in an essentially New Perspective manner, contra Augustine. Even the aforementioned brilliant Pauline scholar John Barclay makes this claim:

> Luther knows very well that when Paul writes of the "works of the law" he is referring to the Mosaic Torah. With Augustine he insists, against Jerome (and in his own day, Erasmus), that Paul does not mean only the "ceremonies" of the Old Testament law, which might be considered simply outdated after the coming of Christ. He means the whole law, including the Decalogue and the moral law of God; and if Paul attacks justification by this, the most perfect law, he would surely include the pursuit of justification by the works of any law.[20]

This quote from Barclay is relevant for a couple of reasons. First it is another witness to the fact that Luther and Augustine understood that Paul was talking about the Old Law, second, you see how even the leading Pauline scholars are under the impression that St. Jerome believed Paul only meant by "works" the old law and its outdated ceremonies. And it is true that if you look at, say, Jerome's commentary on Galatians, you won't find much there connecting "works of the law" with good works. But Jerome wrote more on this subject than is found in that commentary. See what he says in Book 1 of his *Against the Pelagians*:

> Such is the assurance I have through Jesus Christ towards God, not because we are sufficient to think, anything as from ourselves, but our sufficiency is from God, who also has made us fit ministers of the new covenant. For man is not justified by the works of the law, but by the faith of Jesus Christ....The

---

[20] Barclay, 83.

law has been fulfilled by nobody…we are saved, not by the power of the free will, but by the mercy of God…For the goodness and mercy of our Savior have saved us, not by reason of good works that we did ourselves, but according to his mercy.

In the context of an argument with Pelagians, Jerome uses Paul's doctrine of justification to argue we are not saved *"by the power of free will"* nor *"by reason of good works that we did ourselves."* So, while it may be true that Jerome saw Paul as primarily talking about the issue of the Mosaic Law, that did not prevent him from affirming that Paul was also talking about good works. The mere fact that an author exegetes Paul in the former terms does not rule out the latter. The New Perspective is not the claim that Paul was talking about Jews and Gentiles, it is the negation, the claim that Paul was not also talking about good works and earning salvation.[21]

With the previous paragraphs in mind, we turn now to an influential work of recent scholarship, to Dr. Matthew Thomas' *Paul's "Works of the Law" in the Perspective of Second-Century Reception.* Seeking to retrieve the very earliest readings of Paul to compare with the Old and New perspectives, Dr. Thomas looks specifically at whether these early interpreters believed "earning salvation" was the problem with Jewish insistence on the works of the law. Dr. Thomas' effort is of obvious merit, as every Catholic who becomes aware of this debate immediately recognizes the value of the patristic witness. What did the earliest Christians believe? How did the Christians who knew the apostles interpret "works of the law"? Dr. Thomas looked at the *Didache*, the *Epistle of*

---

[21] One response to this point I am making may very well be that I am painting the issue in too stark of terms. The difference between Old and New, they may say, is not of absolute, either/or, interpretations, but rather, one of emphasis: the Old sees the issue primarily in terms of good works, the New sees it primarily in terms of the Jewish law. But the New, they may say, does not rule out entirely the issue of earning salvation. And while certain people who identify as being a part of the New may allow for that issue to be in Paul, by doing so they are actually in the Old. The Old, as I have pointed out, always understood that Paul was talking about the issue of the Judaizers. It never denied that Paul was talking about that. The New takes its departure by denying that Paul was, also, in addition to that, also talking about earning salvation. Still some others may say that there is no single "New Perspective" - and to the extent that each interpreter has their own unique vision, this is true. But this is a trivial point, and the generalization is justified by the history: "Jews were not earning salvation; therefore Paul wasn't arguing against it." i.e., the New Perspective is indeed characterized by the negation.

Barnabas, the *Epistles of Ignatius of Antioch*, the *Epistle to Diognetus*, the *Apology of Aristides*, and works from Justin Martyr, Melito of Sardis, and Irenaeus, and after looking at these works, he concluded that "the new perspective…is corroborated by the early patristic witnesses."[22] The evidence for his conclusion? These authors understood the problem with Jewish insistence on the works of the law in terms of the Mosaic law having been fulfilled, outdated, and replaced by the law of Christ. The Jewish error was insisting on commands that were no longer relevant or binding on the people of God. Only the commands of Christ are now binding. That is what the authors say, and it is on this basis that Dr. Thomas concluded they corroborated a New Perspective reading. But if we stop for a moment and consider whether the aforesaid actually supports that conclusion, we remember that Old Perspective interpreters would agree with all of this: the Old Law was fulfilled and replaced by the law of Christ. Christians have an obligation not to the Law of Moses, but to the commands of Christ. God does not require us to observe Sabbath, but to love our neighbor, to abstain from adultery and greed. Salvation cannot be obtained apart from repenting and obeying God.[23] Luther and Augustine and Old Perspective interpreters agree with all this. Importantly, what Dr. Thomas did not find was a statement from any of these authors that Paul was only talking about works of the Mosaic Law, that Paul was not *also* talking about good works and earning salvation.

A significant issue with Dr. Thomas' book was his methodology used to select texts: he focused only on those that featured a conflict with Jewish people about the law. But most Old Perspective interpreters, in the context of a debate with Jews about the law, would focus on the outdated/fulfilled nature of the old law, and the need now to only follow Christ and his teachings. Is it any surprise that in the context of a dispute with Jews, early Christians were going to be talking about things like the outdated nature of circumcision and the Sabbath? The most ardent Old Perspective interpreter would talk about those things, in that context. And if we asked the authors Dr. Thomas did look at - Barnabas, Ignatius, Aristedes, Justin Martyr, Irenaeus, or Melito of Sardis, etc. - whether Paul's discussion about "works of the law" was relevant, in the

---

[22] Matthew J. Thomas, *Paul's "Works of the Law" in the Perspective of Second-Century Reception* (Tübingen: Mohr Siebeck, 2018), 224.
[23] Augustine and Luther would parse out the necessity of obedience differently, but they both affirmed it was necessary. For Luther, obedience was a natural fruit of true faith, apart from which salvation was impossible. For Augustine, the fruit was not quite as guaranteed by faith but depended more on our continued cooperation with God.

context of a debate with a Pelagian-esque opponent, to the question of human effort, doing and believing, grace and works, earning salvation, etc., it is quite likely they would say it is: that Paul had that sort of thing in mind, too. But Dr. Thomas only looked at texts that reference Paul's "works of the law" in relation to questions about Judaism, and intentionally excluded from the outset any reference that occurred outside that context. Here is his own description:

> With regards to the sources engaged, this study seeks to avoid admitting false positives into its analysis by only engaging contexts which, like Paul's discussions in Romans and Galatians, show evidence of conflict with Jewish parties regarding the law and/or works. This means that texts such as 1 Clement and Polycarp's Philippians are not evaluated, which, though containing general material on justification/salvation and works, show no evidence of conflict with Jews or dispute over the law.[24]

Imagine a first-century Christian, perhaps even one of the first Popes, perhaps even a Saint of the Catholic Church, writing on the subject of justification, utilizing Paul's doctrine to say that no good works of any kind could justify a person, and feeling no need to mention Judaism or do any of the exegetical work connecting the dots from "works of the law" to good works in general, as if the connection was obvious. This would be a deeply Old Perspective reading, and yet, if such a text existed, Dr. Thomas would have excluded it a priori: *"texts…which contain general material out justification/salvation and works, (but) show no evidence of conflict with Jews or dispute over the law" are "not evaluated."* And yet the suggested text is not just an exercise in an imaginary hypothetical. We have a text from Pope Saint Clement, his *Epistle to the Corinthians*, dated as early as the late first century, which does exactly that:

> Therefore they were all glorified and magnified, not through themselves or through their own works or through the righteous deeds which they did, but through His will. And so we, having been called through His will in Christ Jesus, aren't justified through ourselves or through our own wisdom or understanding or piety or works which we did in holiness of heart, but through faith, by which the Almighty God justified

---

[24] Thomas, 18-19.

all who have existed from the beginning; to whom be the glory
for ever and ever. Amen.

This text hardly seems irrelevant to the conclusion that "the new perspective is
corroborated by the early patristic witnesses." This Christian, a Pope and a
Saint, writing near the end of the first century, in perhaps the earliest text
available to us from the post-New Testament era, understood Paul's "apart
from works" in terms of good works, even "works which we did in holiness of
heart", without making any reference to the Mosaic law, and without feeling
any need to explain to his audience why this is an acceptable application of the
text. This is the exact sort of exegesis and application of Paul's words that New
Perspective advocates deny is legitimate. They might agree with St. Clement
that a person is justified apart from good works, but they deny that Paul's
discussion about "works of the law" is a legitimate basis for deriving that truth.
But this is precisely what Clement did, derived good works from works of the
law, derived *sola fide* from Paul.

Another text from this era evidences the same. Saint Polycarp's *To the
Philippians* (ca.120 AD) includes this line: *"by grace you are saved, not of works, but
by the will of God through Jesus Christ;"* 'works' here not being qualified by reference
to the law. Perhaps more interestingly, Dr. Thomas seems to have missed a
couple examples of Old Perspective readings in the very texts he did include.
St. Irenaeus, for example, in *Against Heresies* (4.27.2), picked up the language of
Romans 3 and substituted the "works" in that passage with human ability in
general: *"For all men come short of the glory of God, and are not justified of themselves, but
by the advent of the Lord."* It does not seem that Irenaeus limited the negated
works to merely the outdated works of Jewish law, but thought it applied also
to a person's ability to save themselves (*"of themselves"*). Another example Dr.
Thomas seems to have missed is in Ignatius' *To the Magnesians,* wherein Ignatius
admonished his readers: *"Let us not, therefore, be insensible to His kindness. For were
He to reward us according to our works, we should cease to be."* This statement appears
to be based on Paul's use of Psalm 143 in Romans 3, where the "works" in
question are works qua works ("for all have sinned"); and Ignatius' remark
about *"insensibility to God's kindness"* seems to point in a more Old Perspective
direction as well.

In the *Epistle to Diognetus,* also examined by Dr. Thomas, the problem
with Jewish works is described in terms of spiritual arrogance. The Jews
thought they could offer something to God: *"by supposing that they can give anything
to Him who needs nothing, appear to me in no respect to differ from those who (commit
idolatry)."* The Jewish sacrifices, fasts, etc., demonstrated that the Jews thought
they could give something to God, that they could make God their debtor. Is

it a stretch to say the author of *Diognetus* conceived of the Jewish error in terms of thinking they earned, in some sense, their "salvation," through these sacrifices? They who *"offer these things to God as if He needed them?"* The author goes on to say the reason why God waited so long in history to send Jesus to earth, was because He was waiting until He had *"convinced us that our nature was unable to attain to life"* - i.e., humanity needed to be convinced of its inability to save itself. Only once this inability was recognized, would people then be able to appreciate the sweet exchange brought about in Jesus. The author of the *Epistle to Diognetus* uses Pauline language to discuss the futility of human efforts and the need to be humbled about them to appreciate the gratuitousness of salvation in Christ:

> So that being convinced in that time of our unworthiness of attaining life through our own works, it should now, through the kindness of God, be vouchsafed to us; and having made it manifest that in ourselves we were unable to enter into the kingdom of God, we might through the power of God be made able.

Diognetus is of decided Pauline influence, and Protestants have long pointed to it as proof that "the Gospel" was not wholly absent from the early Church. Though they may be wrong about the implications for their doctrine of imputation,[25] they are not wrong in seeing much of the Old Perspective reading here.

So, we do find the Old Perspective reading among first and second century Christians. But what about the very *first* Christians - those alive during the writing of the New Testament itself? We have evidence of their view in the Bible itself. The epistles to the Ephesians, Titus, and 2 Timothy, all apply Paul's language of "not by works" to good works in general. Some may stop and ask, "Aren't these texts authored by Paul?" Many doubt their Pauline origin, but either way, authored by him or not, these texts witness to the earliest, most authoritative interpretation of Paul we have today. Each of these epistles picks up the Pauline "by faith and not by works" phraseology, and uses it to teach

---

[25] See the chapter on Imputation for more. In short, the "sweet exchange" between my sin and the righteousness of Christ makes just as much sense under infusion as it does imputation, for both of these forms of justification are from God, because of Christ's righteousness, and come to us from outside us despite our own sin and unrighteousness.

that the grace of God received through faith stands in contrast with our own works:

> For by grace you have been saved through faith. And this is not your own doing; it is the gift of God, not a result of works, so that no one may boast. (Eph. 2:8-9)

> He saved us, not because of works done by us in righteousness, but according to his own mercy. (Titus 3:5)

> God saved us and called us with a holy calling, not according to our works, but according to His own purpose and grace. (2 Tim. 1:9)

Even the Epistle of James, so commonly marshaled as evidence against reading Paul's "works" in terms of good works, evidences for us the existence of apostolic-era interpretations that understood Paul in precisely those terms. For St. James wrote that "man is justified by works and not by faith alone" (2:24), and was obviously seeking to correct a misunderstanding of Paul, as if Paul's doctrine of "by faith and not by works" implied that a person could be saved apart from repentance. If people then universally understood Paul's works solely in terms of the Mosaic Law, James would not have had to correct such misunderstandings about good works.

As to exactly how James and Paul can be reconciled, we leave for a subsequent chapter. For now, we remain focused on the history of Catholic interpretation. As we continue looking through various examples, it is important to keep in mind that we are not attempting to show any author's holistic theology of faith and works, but only the specific question of how they interpreted Paul's discussion about "works of the law". That these authors understood Paul in terms of a certain *sola fide*, does not mean their systematic theology was defined by that understanding. Most of these authors, being Catholic, can sometimes sound like James, and other times sound like Paul. Here we are focused only on when they sound like Paul.

Aquinas on "Works of the Law"

Having seen in the previous section evidence of the Old Perspective among the earliest Catholics, including from Pope Saint Clement around the end of the first century, some hints in Irenaeus and Justin Martyr, and a deeply Old Perspective reading in *Diognetus*, we now move to the single most authoritative voice in all of Catholic history: Aquinas. Deemed the "Angelic

Doctor," his work in philosophy and theology is required reading in every seminary. His perspective is therefore of considerable weight in determining the Catholic perspective. In the beginning of this chapter, we saw a claim that Aquinas understood Paul's exclusion of works as targeted only at the ceremonial works and not moral works or good works. There are actually quite a few Catholics, even scholars and self-purported Thomists, who think this about Aquinas, and this is surprising given the abundance of statements from Thomas which say the exact opposite. But some seem to have come across a certain text, out of context, which seems to imply this. The text comes from Aquinas' commentary on Gal. 2:15-16, where he writes the following:

> It should be known, therefore, that some works of the law were moral and some ceremonial. The moral, although they were contained in the law, could not, strictly speaking, be called works of the law, for man is induced to them by natural instinct and by the natural law. But the ceremonial works are properly called the works of the law.

Many have hastily concluded on the basis of this text that Aquinas was a proponent of a New Perspective reading. He does say that moral works cannot be called "works of the law," so if all you had was this text, it's understandable how one could come to that conclusion. But when you look at the passage in context you immediately discover he was in the process of saying something quite different. For when Aquinas says that moral works are not, strictly speaking, "works of the law", he is in the process of reconciling two texts: one, Galatians 2:16, which says *"For we account a man to be justified by faith, without the works of the Law,"* and another, Romans 2:13, which says the opposite: *"the doers of the law will be justified."* Aquinas explains how these two work together by making distinctions between different types of "justification" and different types of "works." Read the full context below (from Aquinas' commentary on Gal. 2:16):

> For we account a man to be justified by faith, without the works of the Law" (Gal. 2:16); However, it is said in Romans (2:13): "For not the hearers of the law are just before God; but the doers of the law shall be justified." Therefore, it seems that a man would be justified by the works of the Law.
>
> I answer that "to be justified" can be taken in two senses, namely, doing what is just, and being made just. But no one is made just save by God through grace.

It should be known, therefore, that some works of the Law were moral and some ceremonial. The moral, although they were contained in the Law, could not, strictly speaking, be called "works of the Law," for man is induced to them by natural instinct and by the natural law. But the ceremonial works are properly called the "works of the Law." Therefore, to that extent is man justified by the moral laws—so far as the execution of justice is concerned—and also by the ceremonial laws that pertain to the sacraments, as their observance is a work of obedience. And this is the way it is taken in the word of the Apostle to the Romans (2:13).

See the following graphic to help make sense of this passage and these distinctions.

Types of Works

| Ceremonial | Moral |

Proper to the law, as they only had force under the law

Proper to nature, not the law, as they have abiding relevance regardless of the law

Types of Justification

Doing justice (evidence)

Being made just (salvation)

Texts which say justification is by works

Texts which say justification is not by works

During the time of the law, it was just to do both the ceremonial and the moral works, but apart from the law, it is just only to do the moral works

Neither kind of works, ceremonial or moral, could ever make a person just, because justification before God is infused through faith, not acquired by works

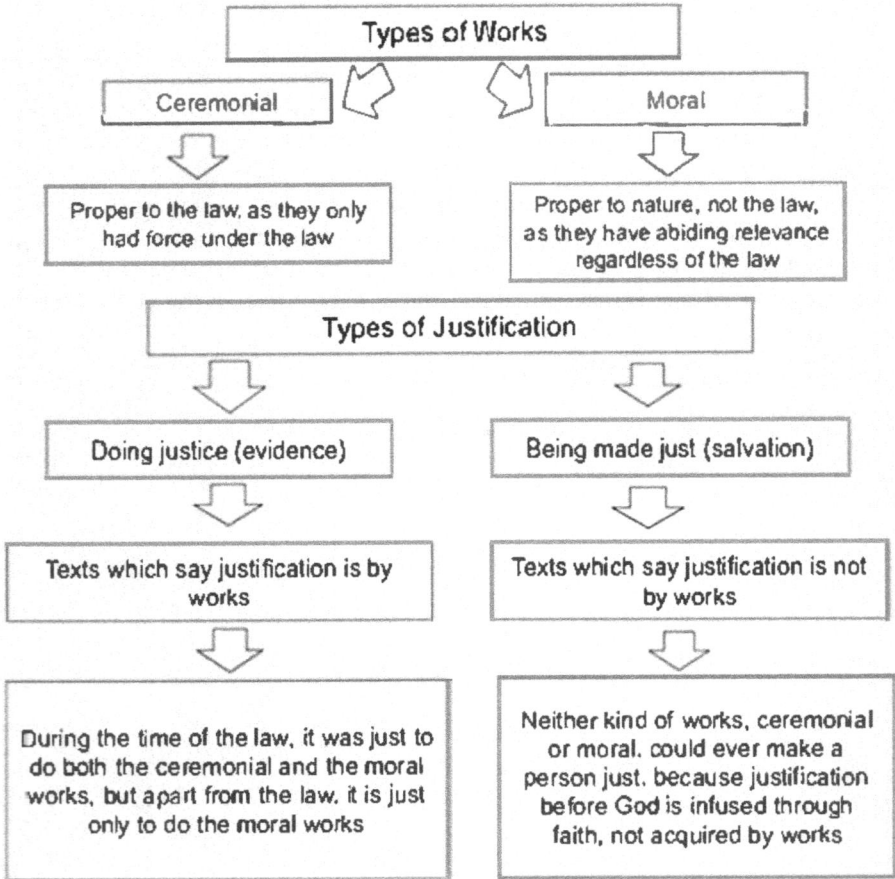

Important here are two types of justification: justification before God (i.e., salvation), and justification in the sense of executing or doing justice (i.e., evidence of salvation). When Paul says in Galatians 2 that we are justified by faith and not by works this is a reference to how we are saved, since grace is not acquired by works but infused through faith. When Paul says in Romans 2 that the doers of the law will be justified, this is a reference to doing justice because obedience to God is a just action. The distinction between moral works and ceremonial works was based on the fact that moral works have intrinsic force in nature regardless of the law, whereas the ceremonial works only ever had force because of, and during the time of, the law. That is why moral works are not strictly works "of the (Mosaic) law": they are works, more fundamentally, of the law of nature.

You will not find a statement anywhere in all of Aquinas to the effect that good works can make a person right with God. Virtually every time he discusses the subject of justification and works, he cites Paul's teaching about works of the law as proof that no works of any kind can make a person right with God. A common rebuttal one encounters to this exegesis of Paul is an appeal to the Epistle of James, wherein it is taught that "*a man is justified by works and not by faith alone.*" Interestingly, Aquinas, aware of this rebuttal, preempts it in his commentary on Galatians 3:

> But against this, it is said in James (2:21): "Was not Abraham our father justified by works?" I answer that "to be justified" can be taken in two senses: either as referring to the execution and manifestation of justice, and in this way a man is justified, i.e., proved just, by the works performed; or as referring to the infused habit of justice, and in this way one is not justified by works, since the habit of justice by which a man is justified before God is not acquired but infused by the grace of faith. Therefore the Apostle says significantly, with God, because the justice which is before God is interior in the heart, whereas the justice which is by works, i.e., which manifests that one is just, is before men. And it is in this sense that the Apostle says, with God: "For not the hearers of the law, but the doers are just before God" (Rom. 2:13); "For if Abraham were justified by works, he hath whereof to glory, but not before God" (Rom. 4:2). Thus, therefore, the conclusion of his reasoning is obvious, namely, that the Law can not justify.

Explaining the Epistle of James in a way that most Catholics would consider an example of Protestant eisegesis, Aquinas says that James cannot mean good works make a person right with God, because justification of that sort is only received by grace and cannot be acquired by works. The justification in James must therefore only be justification in the sense of executing justice, i.e., "doing what is just" (*"which manifests that one is just, before men"*). Aquinas, like Luther, used the Pauline texts that rule out "works of the law" to prove that human works in general cannot make a person right with God, and he does so in the face of other texts which seem to indicate otherwise. What a contemporary Catholic apologist might consider a Protestant work-around of James, is actually the exegetical approach of the Angelic Doctor himself, long before Luther was conceived.

Everywhere we look in Aquinas, he was consistent and explicit about this very thing: when Paul says justification is not by works, Paul is talking about justification before God and is intending to rule out all works, moral and ceremonial (even, we will see later, the commands of Christ). Aquinas says this must be the case because justification of this sort - justification before God - is only infused by grace through faith, not acquired by works. In response to proto-New Perspective claims that Paul was only ruling out the ceremonial works, Aquinas writes the following (from his commentary on Rom. 3:20):

> Now some take the Apostle's words as referring to the first works, namely, that the ceremonials did not confer the grace through which men are made just. But this does not seem to be the Apostle's intent, for he immediately adds: for by the law is the knowledge of sin. But it is clear that sins are made known through prohibitions contained in the moral precepts. Consequently, the Apostle intends to say that by no works of the law, even those commanded by the moral precepts, is man justified in the sense that justice would be caused in him by works, because, as he states below: and if by grace, it is not now by works (Rom. 11:6).

Because Paul says the law reveals sin, we know Paul is not talking about those aspects of the law that are morally arbitrary, like circumcision, sabbath, etc. Paul is talking about the moral law, because that's the law that reveals sin: *'Consequently, the Apostle intends to say that by no works of the law, even those commanded by the moral precepts, is man justified."* And Aquinas says this again in his commentary on Rom. 3:28 - that Paul is not only excluding the ceremonial works, but *"also the works of the moral precepts:"*

> He shows how the Jews' boasting is excluded by the law of faith, saying: for we apostles, being taught the truth by Christ, account a man, whomsoever he be, whether Jew or gentile, to be justified by faith: he cleansed their hearts by faith (Acts 15:9). And this without the works of the law. Not only without the ceremonial works, which did not confer grace but only signified it, but also without the works of the moral precepts, as stated in Titus, "not because of deeds done by us in justice" (Titus 3:5).

In Aquinas' commentary on Gal. 3:10-11, when Paul says, "not by works of the law," Paul is *"speaking here of all works, both ceremonial and moral. For the works are not the cause of making one to be just before God"*:

> The Apostle is speaking here of all works, both ceremonial and moral. For the works are not the cause making one to be just before God; rather they are the carrying out and manifestation of justice. For no one is made just before God by works, but by the habit of faith; not acquired but infused.

In Aquinas' commentary on 1 Tim. 1:8-9, he says Paul is there intending to rule out, not the ceremonial, but the moral precepts:

> For there are in the law certain commandments that are moral and some that are ceremonial... But the Apostle seems to be speaking of the moral precepts, because he continues by saying that the law was made for sinners, and these are moral precepts. The proper use of these precepts is that a man not attribute more to them than is contained in them. For the law was given in order that sin be recognized: for I had not known concupiscence, if the law did not say: you shall not covet (Rom. 7:7). Therefore, the hope of justification must not be placed in them, but in faith alone: we account a man to be justified by faith, without the works of the law (Rom. 3:28).

Of note in the above passage is that he articulates Paul's teaching in the specific language of "faith alone": *"the hope of justification must not be placed in moral works, but in faith alone."*

Moving on to another crucial issue in the debate about Paul: was the apostle attacking an attitude of trying to earn salvation? New Perspective advocates rule this out a priori based on the assumed datum that Jewish people did not think they earned salvation. But we can leave aside for now the question of whether Jewish people were actually doing that, and instead just focus on whether Catholics have read Paul as targeting such an attitude.[26] And Aquinas provides a Catholic reading that does. From his commentary on Romans 9, where Paul says that God chose Jacob over Esau - and this "not because of works" - Aquinas interprets this as an attack on a Pelagian doctrine of merit:

> Then when he continues: "nor had done any good or evil," the Pelagian error is refuted which says that grace is given according to one's preceding merits, even though it says in Titus: he saved us, not because of deeds done by us in justice, but in virtue of his own mercy (Titus 3:5).... He says: in order

---

[26] See the chapter on the Defense of the Old Perspective for more on whether Jewish people thought they earned salvation.

that God's purpose, by which one would be greater than the other, might stand, i.e., be made firm: and this not by reason of merits but according to election, i.e., inasmuch as God himself spontaneously forechose one over the other, not because he was holy but in order that he be holy.

In his commentary on Eph. 2:8-9, Aquinas sees the "not by works" precisely in terms of an attack on human merit and glorying in oneself and one's own actions:

> The second error he rejects is that anyone can believe that faith is given by God to us on the merit of our preceding actions. To exclude this he adds not of preceding works that we merited at one time to be saved; for this is the grace, as was mentioned above, and according to what is written: if by grace, it is not now by works; otherwise grace is no more grace (Rom. 11:6). He follows with the reason why God saves man by faith without any preceding merits, that no man may glory in himself but refer all the glory to God.

And in his commentary on Titus 3:5,

> Then, when he says, not by the works, he states the reason why he saves: first, he rejects the supposed reason; second, he mentions the true reason. The supposed reason is that we are saved because of our own merits. But he rejects this when he says, not by the works of justice which we have done: there is a remnant chosen by grace (Rom. 11:5); not because of your righteousness or the uprightness of your heart are you going to possess their land (Deut. 9:5). But the true reason is God's mercy alone; hence he says, but according to his mercy: the steadfast love of the Lord never ceases (Lam. 3:22); his mercy in on those who fear him from generation to generation (Luke 1:50).

For the Angelic Doctor, when Paul says, "not by works" what Paul means is "not by merits". From the *Summa* (ST I II, 114, 5):

> It is manifest that all merit is repugnant to grace, since as the Apostle says (Rom. 11:6), "if by grace, it is not now by works."

This marks a transition in our exposition of the Angelic Doctor. Up until now we had been looking at his biblical commentaries. But that last quote ("all merit is repugnant to grace, since… "if by grace not by works") was from the Summa.

And to the Summa we now go. For there too Aquinas utilizes Paul's doctrine of justification to argue that human actions in general, moral precepts, etc., cannot justify before God. From *ST*, I-II, 100, 12:

> The latter is true justice, of which we are speaking now, and in this respect of which a man is said to be just before God, according to Romans 4:2: "If Abraham were justified by works, he hath whereof to glory, but not before God." Hence this justice could not be caused by moral precepts, which are about human actions: wherefore the moral precepts could not justify man by causing justice." Hence this justice could not be caused by moral precepts, which are about human actions: wherefore the moral precepts could not justify man by causing justice.

Towards the beginning of this section on Aquinas we said that he understood Paul as ruling out not only the moral works, but also even the works commanded by Christ. Aquinas' clearest statement to this effect is found in his answer to the question, "Does the new law justify?" By the "new law," Aquinas here means the law of Christ, the Gospel. And this is precisely where many New Perspective advocates and Catholic apologists today want to object: whatever Paul might mean about not being justified by works, he cannot be talking about the works commanded by Christ. But Aquinas, picking up an argument from Augustine, argues precisely that point: although the grace of Christ justifies, the works commanded by Him do not. From *ST* I-II, 106, 2:

> There is a twofold element in the Law of the Gospel. There is the chief element, viz. the grace of the Holy Ghost bestowed inwardly. And as to this, the New Law justifies. Hence Augustine says (De Spir. et Lit. xvii): "There," i.e. in the Old Testament, "the Law was set forth in an outward fashion, that the ungodly might be afraid"; "here," i.e. in the New Testament, "it is given in an inward manner, that they may be justified." The other element of the Evangelical Law is secondary: namely, the teachings of faith, and those commandments which direct human affections and human actions. And as to this, the New Law does not justify. Hence the Apostle says (2 Cor. 3:6) "The letter killeth, but the spirit quickeneth": and Augustine explains this (De Spir. et Lit. xiv, xvii) by saying that the letter denotes any writing external to man, even that of the moral precepts such as are contained in

the Gospel. Wherefore the letter, even of the Gospel would kill, unless there were the inward presence of the healing grace of faith.

Aquinas, far from providing support for a New Perspective reading, consistently saw Paul's exclusion of works as an exclusion of good works and an attack on merit. Aquinas directly addressed the idea that Paul only meant the Jewish works, and explicitly says that Paul also intends good works/moral works in general. He even went so far as to rule out works done in obedience to the commands of Christ (for such commands, apart from grace, only kill). For Aquinas, as for Augustine, the "law" in Paul represents not just Judaism and its works, but any moral precept external to man, even the commands of Christ.

Augustine's Perspective

If Augustine is Catholic, then it's a frightening misrepresentation to say that the New Perspective is Catholic. Easily the second most influential and authoritative voice in Catholic history after Aquinas, he anticipated much of the same arguments that New Perspective advocates make today and responded to them some 1,600 years ago. It was the infamous Pelagius, Augustine's opponent on the subject of grace, who inspired the Saint's reflections on this issue. In the view of Pelagius humans already have the grace needed to obey God, and therefore constantly asking God for grace seemed to him to essentially blame disobedience on God (as if He had not already supplied what we need). It was this Pelagian negativity about continually asking for and depending on grace that prompted Augustine's meditations on Paul, and it was out of these meditations that he wrote his seminal *On the Spirit and Letter*, a work in which he draws nearly exclusively from Paul to argue for the necessity of grace and the futility of all human works apart from it.

Taking his jumping off point from 2 Cor. 3:6, which reads, *"For the letter kills, but the Spirit gives life,"* Augustine argued the commands of God (any of them) can only cause condemnation unless grace is supplied along with them. *The letter* - denoting any external command of God - can only condemn, because external commands, even the commands of Christ, do not themselves provide the grace needed to obey. Therefore, the commands of God, insofar as they are external to us, far from justifying us, only make us guilty of transgression. In point of fact, the very reason why God gives commands in the first place is to reveal our sin. Our rebellious hearts, far from complying with the divine decrees, only in response to them, desire all the more what has been prohibited. In light of our guilt and need for grace we are supposed to be driven to Christ, who alone can justify us, and thereby change us into the kinds of people who voluntarily do God's commands out of love rather than fear. The letter of the law kills us, and drives us to the Spirit who gives life.

For Augustine, any obedience, any "works" in observance of any command of God, can only occur *after* a person has been justified, and can never be the means by which they become so. Good works are impossible unless we first have justifying grace dwelling inside us. In order to make this case Augustine depends largely on Paul's discussion about "works of the law", arguing the antithesis between faith and works is more fundamentally about human "doing" and God's grace than it is about the relevance of the Jewish law. He explains that the "law of works" is not simply a reference to Judaism and its works, nor is the "law of faith" simply a reference to Christianity. From Chapter 21 of *Spirit & Letter*:

> The law, then, of deeds, that is, the law of works, whereby this boasting is not excluded, and the law of faith, by which it is excluded, differ from each other; and this difference it is worth our while to consider, if so be we are able to observe and discern it. Hastily, indeed, one might say that the law of works lay in Judaism, and the law of faith in Christianity; forasmuch as circumcision and the other works prescribed by the law are just those which the Christian system no longer retains. But there is a fallacy in this distinction, the greatness of which I have for some time been endeavoring to expose.

Augustine says identifying the works in Paul as simply the old Jewish works is fallacious and hasty. The mere fact that Christianity has done away with the old ritual aspects of Jewish law does not mean Paul was talking about that alone. Augustine admits that might be a natural assumption, but wants to show why it is false. His explanation begins with Romans 7, so it makes sense to share the whole passage here.

> What shall we say, then? Is the law sinful? Certainly not! Nevertheless, I would not have known what sin was had it not been for the law. For I would not have known what coveting really was if the law had not said, "You shall not covet." But sin, seizing the opportunity afforded by the commandment, produced in me every kind of coveting. For apart from the law, sin was dead. Once I was alive apart from the law; but when the commandment came, sin sprang to life and I died. I

> found that the very commandment that was intended to bring
> life actually brought death. For sin, seizing the opportunity
> afforded by the commandment, deceived me, and through the
> commandment put me to death. So then, the law is holy, and
> the commandment is holy, righteous and good. (Rom. 7:7-12)

This passage from Romans is important for Augustine because the particular
command discussed by Paul is the general prohibition against sin, summed up
as *"do not covet."* Augustine presses his audience: how can we say the "law of
works" in Paul refers only to the outdated Jewish law, if what is in view is
actually the law which prohibits covetousness? Is this not also in the law of
Christ? Does not Christ command 'do not covet'? Again, from Chapter 21:

> And so it is the very law of works itself which says, You shall
> not covet; because thereby comes the knowledge of sin. Now
> I wish to know, if anybody will dare to tell me, whether the
> law of faith does not say to us, You shall not covet? For if it
> does not say so to us, what reason is there why we, who are
> placed under it, should not sin in safety and with
> impunity?...If, on the contrary, it too says to us, You shall not
> covet (even as numerous passages in the gospels and epistles
> so often testify and urge), then why is not this law also called
> the law of works?

Because the law in question includes the command not to covet - a command
Christians are required to obey - the issue of faith and works in Paul is not
merely about the outdated Mosaic law being replaced by the commands of
Christ. The rules of natural law that apply to Christians applied all the same to
those under the Mosaic law, and it is precisely those aspects of natural law that
Paul discusses in Romans: the law whose works cannot justify us is the law that
prohibits and reveals sin (Rom. 3:19-20). If Paul is not contrasting faith and
works because they represent two different moral codes, then what is the
contrast about? From Chapter 22:

> What the difference between them is, I will briefly explain.
> What the law of works enjoins by menace, that the law of faith
> secures by faith. The one says, You shall not covet; the other
> says, When I perceived that nobody could be continent,
> except God gave it to him; and that this was the very point of
> wisdom, to know whose gift she was; I approached unto the
> Lord, and I besought Him… the worshipper of God boasts
> not in himself, but in Him. Accordingly, by the law of works,

> God says to us, Do what I command you; but by the law of faith we say to God, Give me what You command. Now this is the reason why the law gives its command — to admonish us what faith ought to do, that is, that he to whom the command is given, if he is as yet unable to perform it, may know what to ask for; but if he has at once the ability, and complies with the command, he ought also to be aware from whose gift the ability comes.

Augustine understands Paul's antithesis between faith and works in terms of an antithesis between grace, humility, and all human "doing" apart from them. The 'law of works' denotes all external commands that threaten punishment, and is intended to drive us to the appreciation of grace. Apart from humility about our inability, and the grace needed to create a new heart within us, both justification and the good works which flow from it are impossible. The commands of God are intended to convict us of these things. The 'law' of faith, on the other hand, is the promise of grace through faith to forgive our sins, justify us, and create a new heart within us that actually accomplishes God's will rather than merely cowering beneath it. Hence Augustine writes that justification is completely apart from any good works or merits, and by the free grace of God. Again, from Chapter 22:

> We conclude that a man is not justified by the precepts of a holy life, but by faith in Jesus Christ — in a word, not by the law of works, but by the law of faith; not by the letter, but by the spirit; not by the merits of deeds, but by free grace.

The antithesis between faith and works is not just between 'doing' and 'believing,' but about grace and merit as well: "earning salvation" is part of what Paul is on about. Again, from *Spirit and Letter* (Ch. 13):

> One who was truly a Jew made his boast of God in the way which grace demands (which is bestowed not for merit of works, but gratuitously), then his praise would be of God, and not of men. But they, in fact, were making their boast of God, as if they alone had deserved to receive His law.

Paul's Jewish opponents thought they were better than the Gentiles, not because God chose them, but rather: *God chose them because they were better.* They alone deserved to be chosen. As an aside here, I (the author, not Augustine) want to point out this consistent flaw with New Perspective exegesis: a failure to think through the whole "pride in being the chosen people" thing. As true as it is, the Jewish people could not have had pride in this if they correctly conceived of it in purely grace-centric terms. But it was their erroneous belief that God chose them because they were better than others, because their works were better than others, that motivated their boasting. God repeatedly rebuked them for this way of thinking throughout the Old Testament (thinking they were chosen because they were better than others), and there is no indication in the New Testament that the Jewish people ever got the message. Students of E. P. Sanders will surely balk, but Sanders admitted as much. See the excursus defending the Old Perspective for more.

Getting back to Augustine, the saint's interpretation of 1 Timothy displays a profoundly Old Perspective understanding of the law and Gospel. For a certain passage in 1 Timothy says two things: both that (1) the law was not made for the righteous, and that (2) the law is good if it is used lawfully. These two statements lead to a confusion, given that the righteous for whom the law is not made, are seemingly the only ones who would use it lawfully (would an unrighteous person use the law lawfully?). In Ch. 16 of *Spirit and Letter*, Augustine unties the knot for us:

> Who but a righteous man lawfully uses the law? Yet it is not for him that it is made, but for the unrighteous. Must then the unrighteous man, in order that he may be justified, — that is, become a righteous man — lawfully use the law, to lead him, as by the schoolmaster's hand, to that grace by which alone he can fulfil what the law commands? Now it is freely that he is justified thereby — that is, on account of no antecedent merits of his own works; otherwise grace is no more grace, since it is bestowed on us, not because we have done good works, but that we may be able to do them — in other words, not because we have fulfilled the law, but in order that we may be able to fulfil the law...The unrighteous man therefore lawfully uses the law, that he may become righteous; but when he has become so, he must no longer use it as a chariot, for he has arrived at his journey's end...
>
> How then is the law not made for a righteous man, if it is necessary for the righteous man too, not that he may be brought as an unrighteous man to the grace that justifies, but that he may use it lawfully, now that he is righteous? Does not the case perhaps stand thus — nay, not perhaps, but rather certainly, — that the man who has become righteous thus lawfully uses the law, when he applies it to alarm the unrighteous, so that whenever the disease of some unusual

desire begins in them, too, to be augmented by the incentive of the law's prohibition and an increased amount of transgression, they may in faith flee for refuge to the grace that justifies, and becoming delighted with the sweet pleasures of holiness, may escape the penalty of the law's menacing letter through the spirit's soothing gift?

In this way the two statements will not be contrary, nor will they be repugnant to each other: even the righteous man may lawfully use a good law, and yet the law be not made for the righteous man; for it is not by the law that he becomes righteous, but by the law of faith, which led him to believe that no other resource was possible to his weakness for fulfilling the precepts which the law of works commanded, except to be assisted by the grace of God.

This interpretation nearly runs the gamut. The law in question is the commands of God generally. And God's commands are not made for people who are already righteous, but for sinners and unrighteous people. The purpose of divine commands is to show us our sin and our need for grace. Once a person has used the law in this way - to understand their inability, and to cling to Christ in faith as their only remedy - they no longer need the law. They are already in grace, they already love God, they are already righteous. The only use of the law which remains is to show others their own inability and need for grace as well, in hopes that they too will be driven to faith. Augustine would make Ray Comfort proud, and his interpretation of "works" is unequivocal: *"Now it is freely that he is justified thereby — that is, on account of no antecedent merits of his own works; otherwise grace is no more grace, since it is bestowed on us, not because we have done good works, but that we may be able to do them."* There is no hint of a New Perspective reading here.

Below is a small collection of quotes which further show the Old, or should we say, Augustinian perspective.

In *On the Grace of Christ and Original Sin* (Ch. 9),

Knowledge of the law, unless it be accompanied by the assistance of grace, rather avails for producing the transgression of the commandment. Where there is no law, says the apostle, there is no transgression; and again: I had not known lust except the law had said, You shall not covet. Therefore so far are the law and grace from being the same thing, that the law is not only unprofitable, but it is absolutely prejudicial, unless grace assists it; and the utility of the law may be shown by this, that it obliges all whom it proves guilty of transgression to betake themselves to grace for deliverance.

And in *On Nature and Grace* (Ch. 4),

This grace, however, of Christ, without which neither infants nor adults can be saved, is not rendered for any merits, but is given gratis, on account of which it is also called grace. Being justified, says the apostle, freely through His blood.

In *Enchiridion: On Faith, Hope, and Love* (Ch. 30),

But this part of the human race to which God has promised pardon and a share in His eternal kingdom, can they be restored through the merit of their own works? God forbid. For what good work can a lost man perform, except so far as he has been delivered from perdition?...And before this redemption is wrought in a man, when he is not yet free to do what is right, how can he talk of the freedom of his will and his good works, except he be inflated by that foolish pride of boasting which the apostle restrains when he says, By grace are you saved, through faith.

Again, in Chapter 31 of the same,

And lest men should arrogate to themselves the merit of their own faith at least, not understanding that this too is the gift of God, this same apostle, who says in another place that he had obtained mercy of the Lord to be faithful, here also adds: and that not of yourselves; it is the gift of God: not of works, lest any man should boast.

In *Responses to Miscellaneous Questions*,

For the Jews desired to give themselves preference over the gentiles who believed in Christ, because they said that they had attained to gospel grace by the merits of the good works that are in the law, and therefore many were scandalized who had believed because of them, because the grace of Christ was being given over to uncircumcised gentiles. Hence the apostle Paul says that a person can be made righteous by faith apart from antecedent works. For how can a person who has been made righteous by faith act other than righteously from that point on, even though previously he had done nothing righteously and had attained to the righteousness of faith not by the merits of good works but by the grace of God, which cannot be lacking in him since now, by love, he is acting well? If soon after having believed he departs from this life, the righteousness of faith remains with him—neither on account of antecedent good works, because he attained to it not by merit but by grace, nor on account of subsequent ones, because none were permitted him in this life. Hence what the apostle Paul says is clear: For we consider that a person is made righteous by faith apart from works.[27]

Again, in the same,

And in the first place I shall seize upon the Apostle's main thought, which is evident throughout the epistle (to the Romans). Now this is that no one should boast of the merits of his works. The Israelites dared to boast of them on the grounds that they had observed the law that had been given to them and so had received the grace of the gospel as though it were due them for their merits, because they observed the law.[28]

From *Sermon 169*,

You see, He was handed over on account of our sins, and rose again on account of our justification (Rom. 4:25). Your justification, your circumcision, doesn't come from you. It is by grace that you have been saved through faith; and this not from yourselves, but it is God's gift; not from works (Eph. 2:8-9). In case by any chance you should say, "I deserved it, that's why I received it." Don't think you received it by deserving it, because you wouldn't deserve it unless you had received it. Grace came before your deserving, or merit; it isn't grace coming from merit, but merit from grace. Because if grace comes from merit, it means you have bought it, not received it free, gratis, for nothing. For nothing, it says, you will save them (Ps. 56:7). What's the meaning of For nothing

---

[27] Augustine, *Responses to Miscellaneous Questions*, eds. Raymond Canning and Boniface Ramsey (Hyde Park: New York City Press, 2008), 140-141.
[28] Augustine, *Responses*, 185.

you will save them? You can find no reason in them to save them, and yet you save them. You give for nothing, you save for nothing. You precede all merits, so that my merits follow your gifts. Of course, of course you give for nothing, save for nothing, since you can find no reason for saving, and many reasons for condemning.

A common theme arises in Augustine's writing: Paul's Jewish opponents were guilty of thinking their good works had merited their election. Paul's antithesis between faith and works is about "doing" and "believing" in general terms. The "law" is not that of Moses but every command of God, and their purpose (i.e., the commands of God) is to convict people of their guilt and inability to obey through their own efforts, and thus drive them to grace. Even in passages like Romans 2, which say *"those who do the law will be justified,"* Augustine will not allow such passages to mean what they say on their surface, but insists on a more careful and labored interpretation - because, in his view, justification cannot be caused by works. From *Spirit and Letter*, Ch. 45:

> Now he could not mean to contradict himself in saying, The doers of the law shall be justified, as if their justification came through their works, and not through grace; since he declares that a man is justified freely by His grace without the works of the law, intending by the term freely nothing else than that works do not precede justification. For in another passage he expressly says, If by grace, then is it no more of works; otherwise grace is no longer grace. But the statement that the doers of the law shall be justified must be so understood, as that we may know that they are not otherwise doers of the law, unless they be justified, so that justification does not subsequently accrue to them as doers of the law, but justification precedes them as doers of the law.

Because works are impossible unless a person is *already* justified, therefore, Paul cannot be saying that works will justify a person, but must be saying that works follow justification. The works are evidence of justification, not the cause of it.

So far in our study of Augustine we have looked only at his topical works and letters. As valuable as they are, it would be inadequate to not look at his biblical commentaries as well. He produced a complete commentary on Galatians but was unable to finish Romans. Now Galatians is friendlier to the New Perspective reading than Romans is (the latter so fundamentally about grace, and not as narrowly focused on the Jew-Gentile issues as the former). If

Romans 3-4 is the stronghold of the Old Perspective, then Galatians 2 is the footstool of the New Perspective. For this reason, it is doubly noteworthy if we find that an interpreter sees *even in Galatians* notes of the so-called Lutheran understanding. While Augustine sees the Mosaic law as more central to Galatians, he still finds in it that fundamental contrast between human doing/inability and the grace of faith that he writes about elsewhere. In his commentary on Galatians, Augustine explains that Paul's opponents had conceived of their own moral goodness and efforts as a work which had made them deserving of salvation. They failed to understand the nature of the grace of the Gospel:

> If then, those who were trying to compel the Gentiles to live like the Jews had also learned what Peter had learned from the Lord - how to be gentle and humble of heart - then at least they would have been drawn by the example of that great man's correction to imitate him and would not have supposed that the Gospel of Christ was a sort of debt paid for their righteousness. Instead, 'knowing that a man is justified by faith and not by works of the law' that is, a person fulfills the works of the law when his weakness is aided not by his own merits but by the grace of God - they would not have demanded from the Gentiles carnal observance of the law but would have known that the Gentiles could fulfill spiritual works of the law through the grace of faith. For by works of the law (that is, if people attribute them to their own power and not to the grace of the merciful God), no flesh (in other words, no person, or none who think in a carnal way) will be justified. And therefore those who believed in Christ when they were already under the law came to the grace of faith not because they were righteous but in order to become so.[29]

Again,

> The law was ordained, therefore, for a proud people so that they might be humbled by their transgression (since they could not receive the grace of love unless they were humbled and without this grace they could not fulfil the precepts of the law at all), so that they might seek grace and not assume they could be saved by their own merits (which is pride), and so

---

[29] Augustine, *Commentary on Galatians*, trans. Eric Antone Plumer (Oxford: Oxford University Press, 2003), 147.

that they might be righteous not by their own power and strength, but by the hand of a mediator who justifies the impious.[30]

The problem with the "works of the law," says Augustine, occurs when *"people attribute them to their own power and not to the grace of the merciful God."* Justification *"*not by works of the law,*"* means *"not by (your) own merits but by the grace of God."*

To be clear, the point here is not to prove that the Jewish people were unique in their pride. I will spend time discussing this in my chapter defending the Old Perspective, but it is worth briefly mentioning here. While there is, contra the E.P. Sanders-based a priori datum of the New Perspective, plenty of reason to believe that Jewish people did think they earned salvation, it is crucial to point out that this isn't unique to Jewish people. Every human is prone to self-righteousness, to thinking they deserve something from God, to thinking they are good, that they are better than others, that all their actions are justified, etc. The Bible is replete from start to finish with rebukes of this sort of thinking: that God chooses us because of our own merits and righteousness. And this is because humanity, not the Jews particularly, is guilty of this.

Getting back once again to Augustine, it was mentioned previously that his commentary on Romans was left unfinished. True as that is, what he completed still provides useful material for the discussion here. In describing the issue that gave rise to the epistle, he writes, *"The Jews thought that the reward of the Gospel had been paid to them for merits accruing from works of the law, and did not want this reward given to the uncircumcised, whom they regarded as undeserving."*[31] Echoing again the accusation that the Jewish people had wrongly conceived of religion in terms of a system of works-righteousness, in which salvation accrues to a person based on their merits, Augustine goes through Romans explaining its contents likewise. The issue here or there in Romans might be the relevance of the Mosaic law, but the underlying problem with the Jewish insistence upon works of the law was a mistaken understanding of their own ability to fulfill it. There is a tendency for people (both Jewish and Gentile) to boast in their own strength and merits, and to pridefully conceive of salvation as something they have earned by good works:

> This argument was used against certain Jews who, once they believed in Christ, both gloried in the works they did before receiving grace and claimed that they had merited this same

---

[30] Augustine, *Galatians*, 167.
[31] Ibid., 127.

grace of the Gospel by their own previous good works, though only the person who has already received grace can do good works…This, the theme of the entire argument, here leads to the conclusion, since Paul taught that we do good by the mercy of God, that the Jews should not glory on account of their works, who, when they had received the Gospel, thinking that this should be attributed to their own merit, did not want it to be given to the Gentiles. They ought now to cease from this pridefulness and understand that, if we are called to belief not through our own works but by the mercy of God, so that we who believe do good, then they ought not begrudge the Gentiles this mercy as though it had been given to the Jews on account of their previous merit, which is nothing.[32]

He repeats more of the same in *Sermon 120*,

But how do the Jews come to be banished from this grace, like foreigners, like refugees? Because they have zeal for God, but not according to knowledge. What knowledge? Being ignorant, he says, of God's justice, and wishing to establish their own (Rom. 10:2-3); only holding on to God in the commandments, and reckoning that they could carry out the commandments by their own powers, they shunned his help. For the end of the law is Christ, the perfection of the law is Christ, unto justice for everyone who believes (Rom. 10:4). And what does Christ do? He justifies the ungodly. By believing indeed in the one who justifies the ungodly, not the godly but the ungodly; making godly the one he finds ungodly; so to the one who believes in him who justifies the ungodly, his faith is accounted as justice. For if Abraham was justified by works, as though he had done it all himself, as though he had bestowed it on himself, he has something to boast about, but not in God's presence (Rom. 4:5.2). But whoever boasts should boast in the Lord, and should say without a qualm, In your justice rescue me and free me (Ps. 71:2). Because he does rescue and free those who hope in him, not attributing to their own powers what they have received.

---

[32] Augustine, *Unfinished Commentary on the Epistle to the Romans*, trans. Paula Fredriksen (Chico: Scholars Press, 1982), 33-37.

Finishing up this section on Augustine's perspective, we end with one last quote, in which he both equates "works of the law" with good works and uses the specific terminology of *sola fide* (faith alone). From *Sermon 2*, commenting on Abraham's justification in Romans 4:

> Abraham believed God and it was reckoned to him as justice, and he was called God's friend. That he believed God deep in his heart is a matter of faith alone. But that he took his son to sacrifice him, that undaunted he took the weapon in his right hand, that he would that instant have struck the mortal blow unless the voice had restrained him, all this is certainly a great act of faith, but also a great work. And God praised the work when he said, Because you have listened to my voice. So why does the apostle Paul say, We reckon that a man is justified by faith without the works of the law? And elsewhere he says, And faith which works through love. How does faith work through love, and how is a man justified by faith without the works of the law? Consider carefully just how, brothers. Somebody believes, receives the sacraments of faith in bed, and is dead. He had no time to do works. What are we to say? That he was not justified? Of course we say he was justified, by believing in him who justifies the wicked (Rom. 4:5). So this person is justified without having done any work. And the apostle's judgment is borne out, where he says, We reckon that a person is justified by faith without the works of the law. The thief who was crucified with the Lord believed with his heart unto justice, confessed with his lips unto salvation (Rom. 10:10). For faith which works through love, even if it has no chance of working outwardly.

As we move through various Catholic interpreters, we will see that they often times struggle to explain how a person could be justified by faith apart from works of the law, and in trying to explain this, they will often, as Augustine did here, refer to the Thief on the Cross as an example of a sinner who did no good works but was saved by faith. That is to say, examples of people being justified apart from good works are used to show how people can be justified apart from works of the law, and this in itself shows that an Old Perspective reading is implicit, even if elsewhere a given author only sees the issue in terms of Jews, Gentiles, and the Mosaic Law.

Ambrose and Ambrosiaster

If one were to conceive of Augustine as the fountainhead out of which the Old Perspective flowed, then it would seem like he came up with that interpretation on his own (some of his detractors claim this, at least). The historical record, however, does not bear out that narrative. For Augustine became a Christian in part because he befriended St. Ambrose, bishop of Milan, and would often listen to him preach. And in the writings of Ambrose, we find what may have been the impetus for much of Augustine's own reading of Paul. For example, in his work on Joseph, Ambrose writes the following,

> And they [the sons of Jacob] began to desire to plead their case to the man who was steward of the house at the door of the house [cf. Gen. 43:19-24]. They still hesitate to enter in and prefer to be justified from their works [cf. Gal. 2:16], for they desire to prove a case rather than to receive grace and so they are refuted at the gates.[33]

The problem with the brothers was they spurned grace, preferring to justify themselves by their own works, wanting to plead the case of their own righteousness. Like a good Lutheran, even in this story from Genesis about Joseph, where nothing about justification, works, or merit is even remotely in view of the original text, Ambrose nevertheless sees an example of that quintessential human sin of works-righteousness and the relevance of Paul's doctrine of justification. Works in Paul for Ambrose denote all works; the law was given to convict us, and to glory in our own works is sin. All deeply old perspective readings. From his *Epistle 73*, section 11:

> God chose that man should seek salvation by faith rather than by works, lest any should glory in his deeds and should thereby incur sin. This is what he says: "By the Law sin abounded, but grace abounded by Jesus" [Rom. 5:20], since after the whole world became subject he took away the sins of the whole world, as John bears witness, saying: "Behold the Lamb of God, who takes away the sin of the world!" [John 1:29] Let no one glory, then, in his own works, since no one is justified by his deeds, but one who is just has received a gift, being

---

[33] Ambrose, "Joseph," *The Fathers of the Church*, vol. 65, 221-22.

justified by Baptism. It is faith, therefore, which sets us free by the blood of Christ, for he is blessed whose sin is forgiven and to whom pardon is granted [Ps. 32:1].

Ambrose believed the purpose why God ordained for salvation to be by faith was to prevent us from glorying in our own works. This is about good works and boasting in personal piety. God gave the law to convict us, to drive us to an appreciation of grace and the blood of Christ which saves us. Faith receives salvation as a gift, not as something we have done, but as pardon for our sins.

Now the writings of a certain "Ambrosiaster" were for a long time considered penned by Ambrose, and for that reason will be considered here alongside his. Writing sometime in the mid to late 300s, this author provides another example of an Old Perspective reading among Catholic authorities. His commentary on Romans 4, shared below, uses the phrase "faith alone" four different times, and repeatedly equates Paul's "apart from works" with not just works in general but with every kind of sinful work:

How then do the Jews believe themselves to be justified through works of the law in accordance with Abraham's justification, when they see that Abraham was justified not by works of the law but by faith alone? Accordingly, there is no need for the law when an ungodly person is justified by faith alone before God. According to the plan of God's grace. The apostle says it was determined by God that when the law came to an end God's grace would require faith alone for salvation...David declares those people to be blessed whom God decreed would be justified before God by faith alone without toil and any observance...Blessed are those whose iniquities are forgiven and whose sins are covered. Blessed is the man against whom the Lord has not reckoned sin. Clearly, those whose iniquities are forgiven and whose sins are covered without toil or any work are blessed, since no works of repentance are demanded of them except that they believe...The prophet is talking in a rather prolix way in praise of the grace of God in order to magnify the gift of God. He created three levels on account of the diversity of transgressions. The first of these levels is wickedness or ungodliness, when the creator is not recognized; the second level consists in committing more serious sins; the third level consists in lighter sins. Nevertheless, he says that these are all wiped out in baptism. With these three levels he has designated the entire body of sin...Because the prophet foresaw the happy time of the Savior's coming, he called those people whose sins are forgiven and covered and not reckoned without toil or any work through baptism blessed.

While Ambrosiaster's commentary focuses on the question of the Mosaic law and Gentile inclusion, there are passages like this where the author understands the discussion in terms of 'faith alone' apart from works of any kind. For Catholics throughout the centuries this author's interpretation carried the weight of Ambrose.

Origen

Origen (ca. 185 – 253), one of our earliest exegetes of Paul, and one of the most influential of the early church fathers, especially in the east, was explicit about his New Perspective reading: Paul was not talking about the moral law commanded by God, but only about those outdated Jewish bits that no longer apply:

> One should know that the works that Paul repudiates and frequently criticizes are not the works of righteousness that are commanded in the law, but those in which those who keep the law according to the flesh boast; i.e., the circumcision of the flesh, the sacrificial rituals, the observance of Sabbaths or new moon festivals.[34]

The above quote is clear enough, is it not? I have seen that passage used by Pauline scholars to prove this case. But this is another example of hasty generalization. While in that quote Origen was explicit that Paul was only talking about ceremonial aspects of the law and not the moral parts, yet an accurate understanding of Origen's perspective is not attained by this passage alone. When we look at everything else he writes on this topic we find that Origen does see Augustinian elements in Paul. For example, in his *Commentary on Romans* (book 3, chapter 9), Origen points to the thief on the cross being justified by "faith alone" without any "good works" as an example of Paul's doctrine:

> He is saying that the justification of faith alone suffices, so that the one who only believes is justified, even if he has not

---

[34] Origen, *Commentary on the Epistle to the Romans,* Books 6-10 (Washington, D.C.: Catholic University of America Press, 2002), 159.

accomplished a single work…Who has been justified by faith alone without works of the law? Thus, in my opinion, that thief who was crucified with Christ should suffice for a suitable example. He called out to him from the cross, "Lord Jesus, remember me when you come into your kingdom!" In the Gospels nothing else is recorded about his good works, but for the sake of this faith alone Jesus said to him, "Truly I say to you: Today you will be with me in paradise." … For through faith this thief was justified without works of the law, since the Lord did not require in addition to this that he should first accomplish works, nor did he wait for him to perform some works when he had believed. But by his confession alone the one who was about to begin his journey to paradise received him as a justified traveling companion with himself.

An example of justification by faith alone apart from good works is Origen's way of proving the legitimacy of justification apart from works of the law: *"Faith alone suffices…even if he has not accomplished a single work…nothing else is recorded about his good works, but for the sake of faith alone Jesus said to him, 'Truly I say to you: Today you will be with me in paradise'"*

Origen says in one place that the works in question are only the outdated works of the Mosaic Law, yet in another place he equates the works with the entire pursuit of righteousness - including chastity, wisdom, and all the other virtues. From his commentary on Romans (again from book 3, chapter 9):

And so, Judaic boasting is excluded, not through the law of works but through the law of faith, which is in Christ Jesus, in whose cross the Apostle boasts. For who will legitimately boast about his own chastity when he reads what is written, "anyone who has looked at a woman to lust after her has already committed adultery with her in his heart"? This is why the prophet also says, "How will someone boast that his heart is pure?" Or who will boast about his wisdom when he observes that it is written, "The world through wisdom did not know God; and therefore God was pleased through the foolishness of what was preached to save those who believe," and again, "God chose the foolish things of the world to confound the And who will boast about his own righteousness when God saying through the prophet, "all your righteousness like the rag of a menstruous woman." The only just boasting then is based upon faith in the cross of Christ, which excludes all boasting that derives from the works of the law.

Of note in the above is that Origen does not conceive of the "Judaic boasting" in terms of a pride in ethnic-privilege, but as boasting in things like personal chastity and works-righteousness. This is a decidedly Old Perspective reading. Origen furthers this identification of boasting with self rather than ethnic righteousness, bringing up the parable of the Pharisee and the Tax Collector as proof that "Judaic boasting" was in things like abstinence from adultery, fasting twice a week, tithing, etc. - such boasting is excluded because justification is by "faith in the cross of Christ" and "excludes all boasting that derives from 'works of the law'". Works of the law are thus understood to include the moral works of chastity, etc., and not just those outdated regulations like Sabbath and Kosher diet. Again, from book 3, chapter 9, of his *Commentary on Romans*:

> In order that what we are saying might become even clearer, we shall cite an example from those which are recorded in the Gospel. "A Pharisee and a tax collector went up to the temple of God. And the Pharisee," it says, "standing in the middle, was saying, God, I thank you that I am not like other men: thieves, the unjust, adulterers, or like this tax collector. I fast twice a week; I give a tenth of everything I possess," and so on. Very possibly the Pharisee was speaking the truth when he said these things; yet in the Lord's opinion this man, who was corrupted by the vice of ostentatious boasting, did not go down from the temple a justified man. Such boasting then, which was coming from the works of the law, is excluded, because it does not embrace the humility of the cross of Christ...And so, Judaic boasting is excluded, not through the law of works but through the law of faith, which is in Christ Jesus, in whose cross the Apostle boasts...who will boast about his own righteousness when he hears God saying through the prophet, "all your righteousness is like the rag of a menstruous woman." The only just boasting then is based upon faith in the cross of Christ, which excludes all boasting that derives from the works of the law.

Origen understands Paul's doctrine of justification in terms of an essentially evangelical theology: before and apart from doing any righteous works, God justifies sinners through forgiving grace, and only out of this soil of justification can the fruit of good works grow. Again, from book 3, chapter 9:

> So then in connection with the forgiveness of iniquities and the covering of sins and [the fact] that the Lord does not impute sins, the Apostle fittingly says that only on the basis that he believes in him who justifies the ungodly, righteousness would be reckoned to a man, even if he has not yet produced works of righteousness. For faith which believes in the one who justifies is the beginning of being justified by God. And this faith, when it has been justified, is firmly embedded in the soil of the soul like a root that has received rain, so that when it begins to be cultivated by God's law, branches arise from it, which bring forth the fruit of works. The root of righteousness, therefore, does not grow out of the works, but rather the fruit of works grows out of the root of righteousness, that root, of course, of righteousness which God also credits even apart from works.

Harkening back to a point made earlier in this chapter, it does not suffice to show that an interpreter read Paul in some passages as speaking only about the Mosaic law, as Origen says about Paul in some places. Everyone on the Augustinian/Lutheran side of the aisle agrees that Paul is sometimes targeting primarily those works. The question is whether Paul ever also intended to target good works and earning salvation. And Origen at times sees Paul as doing just that. There are other interesting aspects of Origen's interpretation, like his varied definitions of law[35], but this suffices for our present purpose.

Chrysostom

After having shown that the two most influential authorities in Catholic history embraced a decidedly Old Perspective reading, it would be easy for some to dismiss this as a symptom of the western introspective conscience. But we just witnessed an old perspective reading from Origen, an easterner,

---

[35] Depending on the verse in question, Origen variously understands the law in question, at times in terms only of the ceremonial law, at times of the entire law of Moses, at times in terms of the entire natural law. This makes good sense of the apostle, but it is an interesting topic for another study.

and of even greater import is St. John Chrysostom, who is both a doctor of the Church and the greatest authority to come out of the East. The golden-mouthed Saint consistently understood Paul's discussion of the "works of the law" in terms of a basic antithesis between human doing and believing, receiving and achieving, and grace and effort. Even when the "doing" is understood in terms of the Mosaic law, the reason why such "doing" is ineffective, in his view, is because it would entail achieving complete obedience to the entire law, i.e., sinlessness: *"there is no other way of becoming righteous in the Law save by fulfilling the whole of it. But this has not been possible for any one"* (from Chrysostom's *Homily 3 on Galatians*). Because all have sinned (because no one has "works"), justification is only available by grace through faith. Hence even when Chrysostom sees the primary question as the relevance of the Mosaic law, his exegesis supports the basic tenets of an Old Perspective reading of Paul. And in his commentary on Galatians he says that those who adhere to "faith alone" are blessed, while those who cling to the law are cursed. From *Homily 3 on Galatians*,

> And this he removes, with great skill and prudence, turning their argument against themselves, and showing that those who relinquish the Law are not only not cursed, but blessed; and they who keep it, not only not blessed but cursed. They said that he who kept not the Law was cursed, but he proves that he who kept it was cursed, and he who kept it not, blessed. Again, they said that he who adhered to Faith alone was cursed, but he shows that he who adhered to Faith alone, is blessed.

In explaining just why those under the law are cursed, Chrysostom points to the universality of sin as the ultimate reason why works cannot justify. In order for justification to come by the law, one would have to have actually "done" it. But no one has done it, for all have sinned. The question is fundamentally about human inability to obey God, and not just about whether the Mosaic Law is still applicable. Because justification by works is impossible due to human sin, an easy way was provided: that from faith (continued from *Homily 3 on Galatians*):

> For all have sinned, and are under the curse. However he does not say this yet, lest he should seem to lay it down of himself, but here again establishes his point by a text which concisely states both points; that no man has fulfilled the Law, (wherefore they are under the curse,) and, that Faith justifies. What then is the text? It is in the book of the prophet

Habakkuk, The just shall live by faith, which not only establishes the righteousness that is of Faith, but also that there is no salvation through the Law. As no one, he says, kept the Law, but all were under the curse, on account of transgression, an easy way was provided, that from Faith.

Chrysostom makes the point simply: because the law requires also works and not only faith - and because works are impossible due to the universality of sin - therefore, salvation cannot come from the law, but only through grace and faith (again from *Homily 3 on Galatians*):

For the Law requires not only Faith but works also, but grace saves and justifies by Faith. You see how he proves that they are under the curse who cleave to the Law, because it is impossible to fulfill it; next, how comes Faith to have this justifying power.

God's purpose of giving the law in the first place was to show us, when we tried to obey it, our own sin and inability to do so. When a person looks to the law as their support, they will only find themselves to be transgressors of it. God intends the convicting effect of the law - the realization of our sin in the face of the commands of God - to be the motivating force which drives people to flee the law and cling to grace. From Chrysostom's *Homily 7 on Romans*,

For if you boast in the Law, he means, it puts you to the greater shame: it solemnly parades forth your sins before you. Only he does not word it in this harsh way, but again in a subdued tone; For by the Law is the knowledge of sin...For the Law accomplished the disclosure of sin to you, but it was your duty then to flee it. Since then you have not fled you have pulled the punishment more sorely on yourself, and the good deed of the Law has been made to you a supply of greater vengeance. Now then having added to their fear, he next brings in the things of grace, as having brought them to a strong desire of the remission of their sins.

In the above passage, the works of the law are equated with a "good deed" ("*the good deed of the Law has been made to you a supply of greater vengeance*"). And in his *Homily 8 on Romans*, Chrysostom likewise understands Paul's 'works' in terms of good deeds:

> But for a person richly adorned with good deeds, not to be made just from hence, but from faith, this is the thing to cause wonder, and to set the power of faith in a strong light.

Every human being wants to claim that they have contributed something to their own salvation, that they are better than others - but attempts to be justified by our own works only magnify our sins. From his *Homily 7 on Romans*,

> And this is why the Apostle here keeps presenting them in turns, and speaks of the righteousness of God being witnessed by the Law and the Prophets. Then that no one should say, How are we to be saved without contributing anything at all to the object in view?...Here again the Jew is alarmed by his not having anything better than the rest, and being numbered with the whole world. Now that he may not feel this, he again lowers him with fear by adding, For there is no difference, for all have sinned.

In the eyes of Chrysostom, the righteousness of God, which Luther so feared before his 'tower experience,' is precisely that righteousness by which God justifies the sinner. Because God justifies the sinner, it is clear that justification is not of works. Hence, again, the question is not merely with regards the Mosaic law, but about human sin and morality in general. The righteousness of God is easy, received by faith apart from whether we have sinned - apart from works (*Homily 7 on Romans*):

> So also is the declaring of His righteousness not only that He is Himself righteous, but that He does also make them that are filled with the putrefying sores (κατασαπέντας) of sin suddenly righteous. And it is to explain this, viz. what is declaring, that he has added, That He might be just, and the justifier of him which believes in Jesus. Doubt not then: for it is not of works, but of faith: and shun not the righteousness of God, for it is a blessing in two ways; because it is easy, and also open to all men.

Righteousness by the easy way of grace and faith, and not by works, excludes boasting in one's own "well-doings", and convicts a man of his inability to save himself (*Homily 7 on Romans*):

> But now that He who should save by faith had come, the season for those efforts was taken from them. For since all were convicted, He therefore saves by grace. And this is why

> He has come but now, that they may not say, as they would
> had He come at the first, that it was possible to be saved by
> the Law and by our own labors and well-doings. To curb
> therefore this their effrontery, He waited a long time: so that
> after they were by every argument clearly convicted of inability
> to help themselves, He then saved them by His grace.

The Jewish people were tempted to boast in their "moderation," as if they
behaved well and abided by the law. But justification by faith humbles us,
showing us that we have no claim to our own salvation; this brings hope to the
sinner, since it makes grace available to all (*Homily 7 on Romans*):

> But what is the law of faith? It is, being saved by grace. Here
> he shows God's power, in that He has not only saved, but has
> even justified, and led them to boasting, and this too without
> needing works, but looking for faith only. And in saying this
> he attempts to bring the Jew who has believed to act with
> moderation, and to calm him that has not believed, in such
> way as to draw him on to his own view. For he that has been
> saved, if he be high-minded in that he abides by the Law, will
> be told that he himself has stopped his own mouth, himself
> has accused himself, himself has renounced claims to his own
> salvation, and has excluded boasting. But he that has not
> believed again, being humbled by these same means, will be
> capable of being brought over to the faith.

Contra the New Perspective, Chrysostom understands Paul's "works of the
law" in terms of an antithesis between an impossible route of complete
obedience to God's commands, and the easy way of faith which excludes all
human boasting in our own good works and efforts. In addition to the quotes
already shared, there are a few more worth sharing, which illustrate the same
points further. From his *Homily 8 on Romans*,

> For he that glories in his works has his own labors to put
> forward: but he that finds his honor in having faith in God,
> has a much greater ground for glorying to show, in that it is
> God that he glorifies and magnifies.

From *Homily 17 on Romans*,

> But this he calls God's righteousness, that from faith, because
> it comes entirely from the grace from above, and because men
> are justified in this case, not by labors, but by the gift of

God…there is no other way of becoming righteous in the Law save by fulfilling the whole of it. But this has not been possible for any one… But tell us, Paul, of the other righteousness also, that which is of grace… what says it? The word is near you, even in your mouth, and in your heart, that is, the word of faith which we preach…this way was easier than that. For that requires the fulfilment of all things (for when you do all, then you shall live); but the righteousness which is of faith does not say this, but what? "If you confess with your mouth the Lord Jesus, and believe in your heart that God has raised Him from the dead, you shall be saved.

And from his *Homily 11 on Philippians,*

"And that I may be found in Him, not having a righteousness of my own, even that which is of the Law." If he who had righteousness, ran to this other righteousness because his own was nothing, how much rather ought they, who have it not, to run to Him? And he well said, a righteousness of my own, not that which I gained by labor and toil, but that which I found from grace…This is the righteousness of God; this is altogether a gift. And the gifts of God far exceed those worthless good deeds, which are due to our own diligence.

Bernard of Clairvaux

The underrated Catholic historian Franz Posset, whose area of expertise is Luther, has written several books on St. Bernard of Clairvaux's influence on the Reformer. Posset has shown that all throughout Luther's life, the Reformer always marshaled Bernard as an example of a Catholic who had taught the truth of the Gospel. The citation given by Luther was usually Bernard's *First Sermon on The Annunciation.* In this sermon Bernard draws upon Paul, preaching on the gift of salvation in contrast with our sin and guilt. Agreeing with Luther about the necessity and goodness of assurance, the Saint encourages his listeners to not only believe that God forgives, but to believe that they themselves have been forgiven, pointing towards two of Paul's statements in Romans for support, including his teaching about justification by faith:

If you believe that your sins can be blotted out by Him alone against Whom you have offended, and to Whom alone sin has no access, "you do well": but advance a step further and believe this likewise, that He has in effect forgiven you your transgressions. Such is the testimony which The Holy Spirit renders in your heart, saying "your sins are forgiven you." And so St. Paul "accounts a man to be justified freely by faith."

Here we see Bernard, the great doctor of the Church, a Saint - the "last Church Father" - interpreting Paul's teaching of justification as having to do, not just with the question of the relevance of the Mosaic Law, but with the forgiveness of sins: the answer to forgiveness from sinful works, is justification apart from works. In his *Sermon on the Song of Songs* (II) Bernard repeats this same thing, explaining justification in terms of an unrighteous sinner being judged righteous (i.e., forgiven) on the basis of "faith alone":

> Your power to make men just is measured by your generosity in forgiving. Therefore the man who through sorrow for sin hungers and thirsts for justice, let him trust in the One who changes the sinner into a just man, and, judged righteous in terms of faith alone, he will have peace with God.

It is no wonder why Luther so liked Bernard. If someone presented the quotes above with no author, it would just as likely be that they were written by Luther or Wesley. Going back to the *First Sermon*, there is another passage there from Bernard, in which human merit is attributed to God's mercy; and a denial of personal righteousness is supplemented by an affirmation that, instead of looking to self for righteousness, we should look to the righteousness of Christ "only" (alone). Instead of our own works or merit, we look to the work and merit of Christ:

> My merit therefore is the mercy of the Lord. Surely I am not devoid of merit so long as he is not of mercy...But would this be my own righteousness? Lord, I will be mindful of your righteousness only...since God has made you my righteousness.

There is here no explicit mention of justification or works, but there is no question regarding the allusion and dependence on Paul's doctrine. No other source in Scripture or tradition than Paul's "faith and works" contains this contrast between our righteousness and the righteousness of God, between our merit and the mercy of the Lord. Though we should be careful here. Bernards affirms merit, but as not coming from himself. It is a merit that comes from God's mercy (*"my merit therefore is the mercy of the Lord"*). This is important Chapter 5, when we discuss the Catholic doctrine of merit.

In a last passage from Bernard, coming again from his *First Sermon*, we receive from the Saint more encouragement on the subject of assurance. In the face of all our sins, the atoning blood of Jesus rises above and overwhelms any accusation that can be made against us. Relying on a statement from Romans (*"he was delivered up for our sins,"* cf. Rom. 4:25) that Paul used to buttress the doctrine of justification by faith apart from works of the law, Bernard uses it to buttress assured forgiveness by the blood of Jesus despite our sins.

> My brethren, these "testimonies are become exceedingly credible." In the first place, I have in the Lord's passion the most conclusive evidence as to the pardon of my sins. For the voice of His blood proclaims aloud in the hearts of the elect the remission of all their offenses. "He was delivered up for our sins," says the Apostle, and we cannot doubt that His death has been more powerful and efficacious unto good for us than our sins have been unto evil.

The Council of Trent

Our comments and exposition with regards to the Council will be brief, and for good reason. It is unfortunately the case that insofar as the Catholic doctrine of justification by faith (alone) goes, the Council took a distanced approach. Defining the word 'faith' in terms of mental assent, it limited the power thereof. In a later section we will look at how the broader Catholic doctrine affirms a *sola fide* properly understood, but here a couple things are worth highlighting. First, when the Council of Trent commented on Paul's phrase from Romans 11, *"if by grace then not by works, otherwise grace is no longer grace,"* it interpreted the phrase "not by works" as denoting all human attempts at good works which occur outside the grace of God. From the sixth session, chapter eight:

> And whereas the Apostle saith, that man is justified by faith and freely, those words are to be understood in that sense which the perpetual consent of the Catholic Church hath held and expressed; to wit, that we are therefore said to be justified by faith, because faith is the beginning of human salvation, the foundation, and the root of all Justification; without which it is impossible to please God, and to come unto the fellowship of His sons: but we are therefore said to be justified freely, because that none of those things which precede justification-whether faith or works-merit the grace itself of justification.

> For, if it be a grace, it is not now by works, otherwise, as the same Apostle says, grace is no more grace.

Given that the Council interprets at least one of Paul's "not by works" statements as referring to good works apart from grace, and not just the specific works of the Mosaic law, it seems rather untenable for a Catholic, faithful to Trent, to assert, along with many New Perspective authors, that Paul's teaching never has reference to good works, but only ever intends to rule out the Mosaic law. Such a position is made even more difficult by the first Canon of the sixth session, which anathematized anyone who says that justification is possible by works of human nature or the law without the grace of God:

> CANON I. If any one saith, that man may be justified before God by his own works, whether done through the teaching of human nature, or that of the law, without the grace of God through Jesus Christ; let him be anathema.

The Council of Trent interprets "works" in terms of all works apart from grace. Even though the Council is generally more hostile to *sola fide* (defining faith as assent, and broadening "justification" beyond Paul's definition - more on that in Chapter 5), it still provides good support for the Augustinian reading of "works of the law," contra the New Perspective.

Contemporary Catholics

In many people's eyes, what matters most, or even what ultimately matters when determining "the Catholic view", is what pre-modern Catholics believed. And until now we have been focused on that. But it is also worth considering what contemporary authors say. While many Catholics engaged in the work of bringing Protestants into the Church attempt to do so on the basis of a New Perspective reading of Paul (contra Protestant soteriology), there are plenty of very strong statements in Contemporary Catholicism that cut against this, supporting the Augustinian reading. Beginning first with the Catechism of the Catholic Church, we see a clear allusion to Paul's "not by works" as denoting works in general:

> 2005: Since it belongs to the supernatural order, grace escapes our experience and cannot be known except by faith. We cannot therefore rely on our feelings or our works to conclude that we are justified and saved.

There is no doubt the Catechism is picking up the Pauline doctrine here as the source of its teaching, and the Catechism backs up its teaching with a plethora of citations, perhaps the strongest of which comes from St. Therese of Lisieux:

> After earth's exile, I hope to go and enjoy you in the fatherland, but I do not want to lay up merits for heaven. I want to work for your love alone... In the evening of this life, I shall appear before you with empty hands, for I do not ask you, Lord, to count my works. All our justice is blemished in your eyes. I wish, then, to be clothed in your own justice and to receive from your love the eternal possession of yourself.

Luther never said it as beautifully. Even the good works of a celibate Catholic nun, receiving daily the Eucharist, devout in all her prayers, a daughter of Mary, are still considered as but filthy rags.[36] The saint abandons any claim to works or merits, instead clinging only to the righteousness of Christ.

Pope Francis recently published an encyclical *Gaudete Et Exsultate*, and in it there is a passage in which he explains both the contemporary Catholic teaching of justification apart from works and its historic basis, relying heavily on an Augustinian reading of Paul:

> The Church has repeatedly taught that we are justified not by our own works or efforts, but by the grace of the Lord, who always takes the initiative. The Fathers of the Church, even before Saint Augustine, clearly expressed this fundamental belief. Saint John Chrysostom said that God pours into us the very source of all his gifts even before we enter into battle. Saint Basil the Great remarked that the faithful glory in God alone, for "they realize that they lack true justice and are justified only through faith in Christ."
>
> The Second Synod of Orange taught with firm authority that nothing human can demand, merit or buy the gift of divine grace, and that all cooperation with it is a prior gift of that same grace: "Even the desire to be cleansed comes about in

---

[36] There is a difference between personally/subjectively considering our works as worthy before God, and our works objectively possessing worth due to God's promise and grace. The Catholic is forbidden from trusting their own works, and as such, the Saint "considers" (subjectively) them as but dirty rags. This is not a rejection of the possibility of objective merit, but a subjective disposition of "empty-hands" which trust in God alone.

us through the outpouring and working of the Holy Spirit." Subsequently, the Council of Trent, while emphasizing the importance of our cooperation for spiritual growth, reaffirmed that dogmatic teaching: "We are said to be justified gratuitously because nothing that precedes justification, neither faith nor works, merits the grace of justification; for 'if it is by grace, it is no longer on the basis of works; otherwise, grace would no longer be grace' (Rom. 11:6)."

The Catechism of the Catholic Church also reminds us that the gift of grace 'surpasses the power of human intellect and will' and that "with regard to God, there is no strict right to any merit on the part of man. Between God and us there is an immeasurable inequality." His friendship infinitely transcends us; we cannot buy it with our works, it can only be a gift born of his loving initiative. This invites us to live in joyful gratitude for this completely unmerited gift, since "after one has grace, the grace already possessed cannot come under merit." The Saint avoided putting trust in their own works: "In the evening of this life, I shall appear before you empty-handed, for I do not ask you, Lord, to count my works. All our justices have stains in your sight."

But it is not just a progressive Pope seeking after ecumenism that makes these statements. The most beloved of conservative traditionalists, Fr. Louis Bouyer, wrote about the impossibility of salvation by human efforts, and the good news of the Gospel that comes by faith on the basis on what Christ has done rather than our own doings:

> For if there is something needed for salvation that has a source other than grace received by faith, we are confronted again with the impossible task of the salvation of man by man. The gospel, however, is the good news that someone else - God in Christ - has done for us what we could not do.[37]

And the most influential and famous of Catholic Pauline scholars of the past century, Fr. Joseph Fitzmyer, commenting on Romans:

> We are thus brought face to face with Paul's basic affirmation: No one "will earn justification by obedience to God's

---

[37] Louis Bouyer, *The Spirit and Forms of Protestantism* (Princeton: Scepter, 2001), 28.

requirements" because "works of the law" in the sense of such perfect obedience are not forthcoming.[38]

Even Jerome

Everyone knows that in contrast with Augustine, St. Jerome knew, along with New Perspective interpreters, that Paul was not talking about good works, or setting up some contrast between human effort and grace, or attacking an attitude which seeks to earn salvation. But what everyone knows about Jerome and Augustine is not what Jerome and Augustine knew about themselves. For both Saints, in their biblical commentaries, say that Paul was talking about the civil/ceremonial works as distinct from moral works. Nevertheless, both Saints, in their debates with Pelagians, applied Paul's doctrine to the question of good works and earning salvation.

Arguing against the Pelagians, Jerome cites a passage from Romans as being about human works in general, with no reference to the Mosaic law (all of the quotes in this section are taken from *Against the Pelagians*, Book 1):

Have you not read, pray, "that it is not of him that wills, nor of him that runs, but of God that shows mercy"! From this we understand that to will and to run is ours, but the carrying into effect our willing and running pertains to the mercy of God, and is so effected that on the one hand in willing and running free will is preserved; and on the other, in consummating our willing and running, everything is left to the power of God.

The above passage is an exegesis of Romans 9, being applied to human efforts in general. Moving on, Jerome cites Romans again, arguing that righteousness doesn't come from ourselves or our own merits, but rather, is the gift of God:

We are then righteous when we confess that we are sinners, and our righteousness depends not upon our own merits, but on the mercy of God, as the Holy Scripture says, "The righteous man accuses himself when he begins to speak," and elsewhere, "Tell your sins that you may be justified." "God has shut up all under sin, that He may have mercy upon all" (Rom. 11:32). And the highest righteousness of man is this —

---

[38] Joseph Fitzmyer, *Spiritual Exercises Based on Paul's Epistle to the Romans* (New York: Paulist Press, 1995), 51.

whatever virtue he may be able to acquire, not to think it his own, but the gift of God.

Jerome again interpreting "apart from works" as meaning apart from merits:

> "For by the works of the Law no flesh shall be justified before Him." There is no distinction of persons: "For all have sinned and have need of the glory of God. They are justified freely by his grace." ...he shows clearly that justice depends, not on the merit of man, but on the grace of God.

Even stronger here (we saw this one earlier in this chapter), justification "apart from works of the law" means "not by free-will," not by anything from ourselves, not by good works, but according to God's mercy:

> Such is the assurance I have through Jesus Christ towards God, not because we are sufficient to think, anything as from ourselves, but our sufficiency is from God, who also has made us fit ministers of the new covenant. For man is not justified by the works of the law, but by the faith of Jesus Christ....The law has been fulfilled by nobody...we are saved, not by the power of the free will, but by the mercy of God... For the goodness and mercy of our Savior have saved us, not by reason of good works that we did ourselves, but according to his mercy.

St. Jerome can comment on Galatians, stating that Paul's "apart from works" is limited to works of the Mosaic law, even citing Cornelius from Acts to show how good works can justify. Yet elsewhere in his writings, especially against the Pelagians, Jerome can quote Paul's "apart from works" and apply it to the question of good works, free will, human merit, etc., without feeling any need to explain how a statement about the Mosaic Law can apply to good works - apparently thinking the connection obvious. Interestingly, it is Augustine (in his work *Spirit and Letter*) who takes the time to explain how one goes from A to B, from Mosaic Law to good works, whereas Jerome merely applies Paul's arguments directly without explanation. Contra the narrative that Jerome was New Perspective and Augustine more Lutheran, it was apparently Jerome who felt that the connection between "works of the law" and good works was so obvious that it needed no explanation; whereas Augustine saw the difficulty and took the time to explain.

Sola Fide Prior to Luther

While not specifically about the meaning of the "works of the law" in Paul, the legitimacy of the phrase "faith alone" is intimately connected to whether Paul was excluding good works and merits from justification, since the "alone" in the phrase functions precisely as a negation of those things. For that reason, we want to provide evidence of the use of "*sola fide*" prior to Luther, and include it here in this chapter and not in the chapter about *sola fide* (for this chapter is about historical issues while the other is about theology). Now one of the arguments often made against *sola fide* is that Paul never uses the phrase, and that Luther actually added the word "alone" to his translation of Romans to better fit his theology. However, that argument both betrays a naivety about the possibility of literal translation and about the historical use of the phrase. Of course, one might argue that there is nothing in Paul that justifies the addition of the word "alone", but that argument doesn't have much teeth in a Catholic context where men like Aquinas described Paul's meaning by making that same addition themselves.

Aquinas (*Commentary on 1 Timothy*):

> For there are in the law certain commandments that are moral and some that are ceremonial... But the Apostle seems to be speaking of the moral precepts... the hope of justification must not be placed in them, but in faith alone: we account a man to be justified by faith, without the works of the law (Rom. 3:28).

Chrysostom (*Homily 3 on Galatians*):

> They said that he who kept not the Law was cursed, but he proves that he who kept it was cursed, and he who kept it not, blessed. Again, they said that he who adhered to Faith alone was cursed, but he shows that he who adhered to Faith alone, is blessed.

Origen (*Commentary on Romans*: book 3, chapter 9):

> He is saying that the justification of faith alone suffices, so that the one who only believes is justified, even if he has not accomplished a single work...Who has been justified by faith alone without works of the law? Thus, in my opinion, that thief who was crucified with Christ should suffice for a suitable example. He called out to him from the cross, "Lord

Jesus, remember me when you come into your kingdom!" In the Gospels nothing else is recorded about his good works, but for the sake of this faith alone Jesus said to him, "Truly I say to you: Today you will be with me in paradise."

Bernard (*Sermon on the Song of Songs* II):

Your power to make men just is measured by your generosity in forgiving. Therefore the man who through sorrow for sin hungers and thirsts for justice, let him trust in the One who changes the sinner into a just man, and, judged righteous in terms of faith alone, he will have peace with God.

Ambrosiaster (*Commentary on Romans 4*):

How then do the Jews believe themselves to be justified through works of the law in accordance with Abraham's justification, when they see that Abraham was justified not by works of the law but by faith alone? Accordingly, there is no need for the law when an ungodly person is justified by faith alone before God. According to the plan of God's grace. The apostle says it was determined by God that when the law came to an end God's grace would require faith alone for salvation.

Augustine (*Sermon 2*):

Abraham believed God and it was reckoned to him as justice, and he was called God's friend. That he believed God deep in his heart is a matter of faith alone. But that he took his son to sacrifice him…(was) a great work. And God praised the work when he said, "Because you have listened to my voice." So why does the apostle Paul say, We reckon that a man is justified by faith without the works of the law?... Consider carefully just how, brothers. Somebody believes, receives the sacraments of faith in bed, and is dead. He had no time to do works. What are we to say? That he was not justified? Of course we say he was justified, by believing in him who justifies the wicked (Rom. 4:5). So this person is justified without having done any work.

A fuller list of the authors who used *sola fide* prior to Luther includes Hilary, Basil, Cyril of Alexandria, Theophylact, Theodoret, and Marius

Victorinus.[39] Let no one say that the phrase "faith alone" was novel with Luther: it has a long Catholic history prior to him, and a deeply Catholic nature when understood properly. For the proper understanding of *sola fide*, we devote another chapter. The historical validity and Catholic nature of the phrase is demonstrated here.

False Positives?

The examples set forth in this chapter are not intended to be exhaustive, neither in terms of the number of Catholic authors who understood Paul in an Old Perspective manner (there are plenty left unmentioned), nor, and especially not, in terms of the witness of any individual author. First, when it comes to biblical interpretation, I have presented select quotations from each author wherein they understand Paul's doctrine of justification in terms of good works and earning salvation. This does not mean, of course, that these authors understood Paul to be always and only talking about those things. As we pointed out, even Luther understood that Paul was first addressing the question of Gentile inclusion and the Mosaic Law. Luther nevertheless placed the emphasis on the question of earning salvation. But within the spectrum of Old Perspective readings, the emphasis can vary from Luther, to Augustine, to Chrysostom, to Jerome. The extent to which Paul is talking about good works can be seen to be relatively minor, and yet this still qualifies as an Old Perspective reading. Many of these authors, if told to write only one thing about justification in Paul, would probably choose the fact that Christians receive it apart from doing the Mosaic Law. But as long as they agree that, at least in some places, Paul is also, at least in some way, also talking about earning salvation, then they still land more in that Old Perspective camp (the New Perspective being defined, remember, by its negation of this element).

Second, these citations are mostly examples of biblical exegesis. There is an occasional quote from a theological work, but even there, the quote does not represent the fullness of the author's soteriology. It is only being used to show that this particular element - *sola fide* - is present at times. If we were to display any of these authors' systematic treatment of justification, they would not sound anywhere near as much like Luther as they do in these quotes shared here. While the authors here affirm an antithesis between faith and works, elsewhere they will insist that the two must be joined. Even someone like

---

[39] Joseph Fitzmyer, *Romans: A New Translation with Introduction and Commentary* (New York: Yale University Press, 1993), 360-362.

Augustine, so forceful about human inability to merit and to do good apart from grace, will in some places speak of salvation precisely in terms of merit, earning, and being achieved by human effort. The same is true for all of the authors presented here. The Fathers, like the Scriptures themselves, can say "yes and no," by works and not by works, *sola fide* and merit, at the same time, in different ways. The purpose, then, of this present chapter - which is now about to come to a close - is not to claim that any of these authors understood salvation in terms of *sola fide*, in terms of an antithesis between doing and believing, *in such a way,* that they never elsewhere also expressed salvation precisely in terms of "doing", precisely in terms of merit. All these authors can, and will, in other places throughout their writings, especially in their systematic theologies, parse out faith and works in ways which seem to run contrary to their language here, and to that point we will proceed in the later chapter on *Dialectic.*

Excursus 1
A Defense of the Old Perspective

The previous chapter made what should be, for Catholics at least, a fairly convincing case for an essentially 'Old Perspective' reading of Paul. The Saints, however, were not interacting with New Perspective scholars. I will seek to do that here, offering my own defense of the Old Perspective in dialogue with the arguments and assumptions of the New Perspective. To start with, the initial impetus and foundation of the New Perspective is the idea that Jewish people knew they were elected by grace and didn't think they earned salvation. "Because Jews didn't think that, Paul wasn't arguing against it." This negation results in a reading of Paul that focuses solely on salvation-historical issues about Gentile inclusion, the Judaizers, and the Mosaic Law. And to the New Perspective's credit, those were indeed the questions which prompted Paul to expound the doctrine of justification. But the answer Paul gave to those questions was not simply that the old law was temporary, fulfilled by Christ, such that Jews and Gentiles come together as one people apart from Torah-observance. Paul does of course make that argument, but he goes beyond those things, and in some places grounds his arguments in more fundamental issues about human sin, inability, and pride - setting these things in contrast with grace, faith, and humbly entreating the divine mercy. But why would Paul make those arguments if his Jewish audience already understood them?

There are good reasons to think Jewish people did have a problem thinking they earned salvation, but for the sake of argument, let's say we could go back and survey every Rabbi, and we found that 100%, without exception, all taught in good Lutheran fashion, that trying to earn salvation was an expression of self-righteousness and pride, and that only the empty-hand of faith could receive the grace of God. Would that mean the Jewish people understood it, took it to heart, and had no need of being taught it afresh? A contemporary issue can help shed light. We know that conservative churches around the world nearly unanimously affirm the sinfulness and dangers of pornography. But do conservative Christians therefore have no problem with pornography? We know as a matter of fact they do - even in those churches with clear and consistent preaching on the topic. Now if trusting your works is a real sin, that real people are actually tempted to commit, there is no reason to think that just because Jewish people preached against it, that they therefore didn't need to hear preaching against it. Even in churches that preach the Gospel nearly exclusively in terms of a prohibition against thinking you earn salvation, evangelicals still find themselves regularly tempted with trying to earn, and thinking they deserve, God's grace.[40] The Rabbis in Paul's day might have preached on the unmerited nature of grace with fervor, but that would not mean the on-the-ground appreciation of that truth was what it should be. Stephen Westerholm has an insightful remark on this point, about not letting Judaism's self-understanding limit what Paul says in response to it:

> Paul must not be allowed to be our main witness for Judaism, nor must Judaism, or the position of Paul's opponents, determine the limits within which Paul is to be interpreted. The basis for Paul's rejection of the law must not be determined solely by asking what his foes were proposing any more than we may see Judaism's own perspective of the law in Paul's rejected version of it.[41]

Even if Jewish people understood their faith in terms of unmerited grace (and we will see this isn't quite the case), that should not create an a priori obstruction to reading Paul as attacking a doctrine of merit - especially when his arguments quite explicitly do. The Jewish people may have understood their doing of the works of the law in terms of a humble recognition of, and response to, their gracious election into the covenant; But Paul's rejection of the works of the law is clearly based, at least in part, and at least in some places, on his claim that an insistence on works amounts to an attitude of self-righteous pride - regardless of whether the person doing the insisting was aware of it or not. No religious person would want to admit, not even to themselves - perhaps most especially not to themselves - such a thing about themselves.

To the extent New Perspective advocates will agree Paul is attacking pride, they want to confine the pride to a sense of ethnic privilege - to a Jewish boast of being chosen by God over against the Gentiles, and this, they say, by grace. And many of Paul's statements about justification "not by works" are followed up by statements about Gentile inclusion. Take for example Rom. 3:28-29, *"Therefore we conclude that a man is justified by faith apart from the works of the law. Or is God the God of the Jews only? Is he not God the Gentiles? Yes, of Gentiles also."* If justification was by works of the law, then it would imply ethnic exclusivity…

---

[40] Interestingly, in good Romans 7 fashion, we actually tend to see more of this in Churches that preach against it, than in those that do not. But perhaps it would be more accurate to say people who hear preaching on the subject are more cognizant of the problem than those who do not.

[41] Stephen Westerholm, *Israel's Law and the Church's Faith* (Grand Rapids: Eerdmans, 1988), 150.

God would be the God of the Jews only. But justification apart from works means God is the God of both Jew and Gentile. Therefore, New Perspective advocates tell us, "not by works" has to do with ethnicity rather than ethics. But this is key: for ancient people, especially ancient Jews, ethnicity was intrinsically connected to ethics. To say, in the ancient world, "not by good works", was to include those idolatrous, fornicating, Gentile sinners, too. God being the God of the Jew only, meant God being the God of the good people, the righteous people, the holy people. While it is true that Jewish people had a doctrine of election by grace, their constant temptation was thinking the reason God chose to grace them in the first place, and not the Gentiles, was because they were morally superior. They had merited their election by their good deeds and righteousness. While New Perspective advocates will want to stop right here and protest, by reference to the work of E.P. Sanders, it is actually E.P. Sanders himself who told us, in the opening chapters of his book, that when it came to explaining why God chose the Jews in the first place, the usual answer given by the Rabbis was that the Jews had merited the grace of God because of their ethical superiority compared to the other nations.

The section in Sanders' seminal book devoted to this subject is entitled "The Election and the Explanations of It."[42] There we read that the dominant way *"the Rabbis explained God's choice of Israel (was) by reference to meritorious action by the ancestors;"*[43] and in terms of *"Israel's moral superiority to other nations."*[44] One example comes from a text from Mek. Pisha 5 (to 12.6):

> For one cannot obtain rewards except for deeds. Rabbi Eleazar he-Kappar says: Did not Israel possess four virtues than which nothing in the whole world than which nothing in the world is more worthy: that they were above suspicion in regards to chastity and in regard to tale bearing, that they did not change their names and they did not change their language.[45]

The deeds of the Jewish people is what merited the exodus (from pgs. 88-92 of Sanders' work):

> Because of the merit of the deed which Abraham their father did, I will divide the sea for them. The faith with which they

---

[42] Sanders, *Paul and Palestinian Judaism*, 88.
[43] Ibid., 91-91.
[44] Ibid, 88.
[45] Ibid, 89.

believed in me is deserving that I should divide the sea for them.

The Jews were chosen over against the other nations because they alone were worthy and willing to obey God (again from pgs. 88-92 of Sanders' work):

> When the holy one, blessed be he, revealed himself to give Torah to Israel, he revealed himself not to Israel alone, but to all the nations. He came first to the sons of Esau and said to them, "You accept the Torah." They said to him, "What is written in it?" He answered, "Thou shalt not murder.' They answered that the very nature of their father was that he killed.

> "When the most high gave the nations their inheritance, when the Holy One, blessed be He, gave Torah to Israel, He stopped, looked into the future, and perceived, and there being no nation among the nations worthy to receive the Torah except Israel, he fixed the bounds of the people."

The necessity of the Jews "meriting redemption" is what prompted God to assign them religious "duties" which enabled them to become "worthy of redemption" (again, from pgs. 88-92):

> As yet they had no religious duties to perform by which to merit redemption... "thou was naked and bare" which means bare of any religious deeds. Therefore the holy one, blessed be he, assigned them two duties, the duty of paschal sacrifice and the duty of circumcision, which they performed so as to be worthy of redemption.

The thrust of Sanders work argues that Jewish people did not think they earned salvation, but when you read the work for yourself, you see he admits from the start they believed they earned their election. Sanders wants us to grant the Rabbis the ability to be nuanced in this, to have a doctrine of grace-based merit, arguing that their nuanced view of grace and merit has solid biblical grounds:

> At one time the Rabbis can say that Israel merited the reward of the exodus...while at others they can say that Israel did not have any merits...The Rabbis did not have the Pauline/Lutheran problem of works-righteousness, and so felt no embarrassment at saying that the exodus was earned...grace and merit did not seem to them to be in

contradiction to each other, and doubtless they had good biblical support here.[46]

The quote above is particularly illuminative, especially considering the entire sweep of the present book you are reading (my book: *Sola Fide & Merit*, not Sanders). So far in this book we have been defending an Old Perspective reading, which is at least in part dependent on the idea that Jewish people thought they merited salvation. But in the climactic chapter I will be arguing that *sola fide* and merit are not only compatible, but actually form the biblical and Catholic dialectic of salvation. In the quote above E.P. Sanders agrees both that Jewish people thought they earned their election and that there is a biblical doctrine of grace-based merit. Sanders is, in my estimation, correct: these two things, grace and merit, do have a biblical basis, and can and should coexist in a well-rounded biblical theology. But getting back to our point here, the Jewish people did, even in their explicit theology (and not just in their subconscious), think they earned/merited their election. The Jewish people did not say, "we are privileged over the Gentiles because God chose us," but "God chose us instead of the Gentiles because we deserved it more than they did." It was not "we are holy because we were chosen," but "God chose us because we are holy." God rebuked the Israelites for this way of thinking all the way back in Deut. 9:4-6:

> Do not say in your heart when the Lord your God has driven them away from you, "Because of my righteousness the Lord has brought me in to take possession of this land." ...It is not because of your righteousness or the uprightness of your heart that you are going in to take possession of their land...it is not because of your righteousness that the Lord your God is giving you this good land to possess, for you are a stubborn people.

One might argue: because God told the Israelites this back in Deuteronomy, they surely would have known and appreciated this truth. "Judaism always taught election by grace; therefore, the Jews always knew this, and never had a problem with it" (so reasons the New Perspective). Yes, Judaism (as revealed by Yahweh) always taught grace, but Judaism (as taught and understood by many Jews) failed to appreciate this point. The story of Israel was not one of taking to heart God's messages - nor is that how the story of the Church has gone, either. The people of God do not have a history of immediately taking to heart God's lessons. We are a stubborn people, and to this day we resist the

---

[46] Ibid, 100.

message of our Lord, and need to be rebuked and taught afresh from the Sermon on the Mount every Sunday. The Jewish people were of course no different from us in this regard. All throughout the Old Testament, God had to repeatedly remind the Israelites that His blessings came to them *"not by might, nor by power, but by my Spirit, says the Lord Almighty"* (Zech. 4:6). The constant human temptation is to puff oneself up, to lean on one's own strength… to flatter oneself that you are good, that you are deserving, that you aren't as bad as the other guy. Self-righteousness is, indeed, the human sin par excellence. We want to be like God (Gen. 3:5), we want to build for ourselves a tower to Heaven.

Whether New Perspective scholars think second-temple Jews had a problem with self-righteousness, there is plenty of evidence our Lord thought they did. All throughout the ministry of Jesus, our Lord was in constant confrontation with the Pharisees. Those poisonous spiritual leaders' influence spread far and wide. Our Lord describes them as having led Israel astray. They were supposed to be shepherds, but due to their malpractice, the flock was *"harassed and helpless, like sheep without a shepherd"* (Matt. 9:36). The religious leaders were legalistic hypocrites, show-boaters that took pride in their reputation as holy men and considered themselves superior to others:

> They tie up heavy burdens and lay them on people's shoulders, but they themselves are unwilling to move them with so much as their finger. And they do all their deeds to be noticed by other people; for they broaden their phylacteries and lengthen the tassels of their garments. And they love the place of honor at banquets, and the seats of honor in the synagogues, and personal greetings in the marketplaces, and being called Rabbi by the people. (Matt. 23:4-7)

The people of Israel in the time of Jesus and Paul were being led by a group of men who tended to place an emphasis on the externals of religion without paying due attention to the heart. They tithed 10% of all their goods, down to even their garden herbs, but they neglected justice, mercy, and faithfulness. They washed the outside of the cup, but left the inside dirty. They looked down on others, merely paid lip service to the grace of God, and sought to justify themselves by their own actions. New Perspective scholars tell us it would be historically inappropriate for Paul to set up a doctrine of justification that contrasted trusting your good works and trusting grace, but the only parable our Lord ever taught on "justification" explicitly contained that very antithesis:

> To some who were confident of their own righteousness and looked down on everyone else, Jesus told this parable: Two men went up to the temple to pray, one a Pharisee and the other a tax collector. The Pharisee stood by himself and prayed: "God, I thank you that I am not like other people— robbers, evildoers, adulterers—or even like this tax collector. I fast twice a week and give a tenth of all I get."
>
> But the tax collector stood at a distance. He would not even look up to heaven, but beat his breast and said, "God, have mercy on me, a sinner."
>
> I tell you that this man, rather than the other, went home justified before God. For all those who exalt themselves will be humbled, and those who humble themselves will be exalted. (Luke 18:9-14)

In this parable we see two contrasting examples: a religious Jew paying lip service to God, but actually trusting their own good works; and a sinner simply trusting in God's mercy. Of the two of these, both seeking after a law of righteousness - one guilty of religious pride and works-righteousness, the other leaning on the grace of faith - only one of them attains what they sought (cf., Rom. 9:30-31). Only one goes home justified: *"I tell you that this man, rather than the other, went home justified before God. For all those who exalt themselves will be humbled, and those who humble themselves will be exalted."* Now if our Lord saw fit to address justification in terms of such an antithesis, why should we think Paul's explicit antithesis between faith and works isn't in the same mold? There was, as evidenced by the parable of our Lord, a problem at that time of people trusting good works while paying lip service to grace, and there was a need for the Christian message to rebuke that tendency and contrast trusting good works with trusting God. The message of justification as a gift of mercy to the sinner received through faith, in contrast with the legalistic pharisee who thinks they earn salvation… this was a message that our Lord taught. A message which needed to be taught then, as well as today.

My readers well-versed in the New Perspective may respond: "of course, the theology of many Pharisees was legalistic, etc., but that did not characterize Jewish people as a whole." But the Old Perspective does not depend on the idea that every Jew was trying to earn salvation. Not even Martin Luther would have accused King David, the Prophet Isaiah, Saint John the Baptist, etc., of thinking they earned salvation. Of course, there were many good Jewish people who understood and appreciated grace. But Paul's interlocutors were not good Jewish people. He was arguing against the theology of the *"brood of vipers"* (Matt. 12:34) who condemned our Lord to death, *"the dogs, the evil workers, the circumcision"* (Phil. 3:2). Paul's interlocutor was not the theology of Moses, but the spiritual influence of the Jewish sect our Lord calls *"the synagogue of Satan, who claim to be Jews but are not"* (Rev. 3:9). The people who spread the false doctrine were not guilty of a mere trifle. They were promoting a behavior - seeking justification by works of the law - that would sever a person from Christ (Gal. 5). While it is true that there was widespread teaching on grace, it is also true that there was an insidious theology influencing people contra grace. Even Pharisees may have spoken well on the subject, but their example taught otherwise: *"do and observe whatever they tell you, but not the works they do. For they preach, but do not practice"* (Matt. 23:3).

When Paul argues against works of the law, he does not just say the works are outdated. He *also* says works qua works are ineffective, and contrary to grace when motivated by a self-righteous attitude. The works in question are not always Torah-works, but at times are good works, even all human works in general. Take for example Paul's argument in Romans 9-10. In the middle of Chapter 9 (vss. 11-12) he discusses the calling of Jacob and Esau using the "not by works" phraseology, saying that *"before the twins were born or had done anything good or bad—in order that God's purpose in election might stand: not by works but by him who calls—she was told, "The older will serve the younger."* Paul has defined "works" in the most general terms: *"anything good or bad"* and *"before they were born"* - this is apart from any and every possible work. God's choice had nothing to do with behavior, it was made before they were born, before there was any behavior to base the choice on. A person's calling and election, Paul concludes, *"does not, therefore, depend on human desire or effort, but on God's mercy."* (vs. 16). This is human actions and human effort in the abstract. Later on in the same chapter the subject of Jews and Gentiles comes up, as his audience is wondering why, if Jesus is the Jewish Messiah, have so many Gentiles come to faith while so many Jewish people have not? He answers:

> What then shall we say? That the Gentiles, who did not pursue righteousness, have obtained it, a righteousness that is by faith; but the people of Israel, who pursued the law as the way of righteousness, have not attained their goal. Why not? Because they pursued it not by faith but as if it were by works. (Rom. 9:30-32)

The problem with the Jewish people who failed to come to faith in Christ was not the law they were pursuing, but the way they were pursuing it: as if it could be attained by works rather than by faith. Elsewhere Paul focuses on the law being pursued (the Mosaic law), but here he focuses on something else. The focus here is on a peculiar understanding of righteousness - the understanding common to those Jews who had rejected Jesus - that it was something established by their own works. They wanted to establish their own righteousness: *"they are zealous for God, but their zeal is not based on knowledge. Since they did not know the righteousness of God and sought to establish their own, they did not submit to God's righteousness"* (Rom. 10:2-3). In response to Jewish attempts to establish their own righteousness, as if it were something attained by works rather than by faith, Paul contrasts the two ways of righteousness, recalling the rebuke God offered self-righteousness back in Deuteronomy 9:

> Moses writes this about the righteousness that is by the law: "The person who does these things will live by them." But the righteousness that is by faith says: "Do not say in your heart, 'Who will ascend into heaven?' (that is, to bring Christ down) or 'Who will descend into the deep?' (that is, to bring Christ up from the dead)." But what does it say? "The word is near you; it is in your mouth and in your heart," that is, the message concerning faith that we proclaim. (Rom. 10:5-8)

The first way of righteousness - that by the law - depends on one's own "doing" of the law. But Paul has already said that no one can be justified by the law, because the law reveals sin, i.e., when anyone compares themselves to the law, they find themselves a sinner, because no one has actually done the law (*"No, not a single one,"* Rom. 3:10). Clearly the first way of righteousness - that by doing - is impossible. The second way of righteousness - that by faith - is buttressed by passages from Deuteronomy 9 and Deuteronomy 30. See the following graphic and explanatory comments below it.

Deuteronomy 9:4	Romans 10:3-8
When the Lord your God thrusts them out before you, <u>do not say in your heart</u>, "It is because of <u>my righteousness</u> that the Lord has brought me in to occupy this land." **Deuteronomy 30:11-14** Now what I am commanding you today is not too difficult for you or beyond your reach. It is not up in heaven, so that you have to ask, "<u>Who will ascend into heaven</u> to get it and proclaim it to us so we may obey it?" Nor is it beyond the sea, so that you have to ask, "Who will cross the sea to get it and proclaim it to us so we may obey it?" No, <u>the word is very near you; it is in your mouth and in your heart</u> so you may obey it.	Since they did not know the righteousness of God and <u>sought to establish their own</u>, they did not submit to God's righteousness. Christ is the culmination of the law so that there may be righteousness for everyone who believes. Moses writes this about the righteousness that is by the law: "The person who does these things will live by them." But the righteousness that is by faith says: <u>Do not say in your heart</u>, "<u>Who will ascend into heaven?</u>" (that is, to bring Christ down) or "Who will descend into the deep?" (that is, to bring Christ up from the dead). But what does it say? "<u>The word is near you; it is in your mouth and in your heart</u>," that is, the message concerning faith that we proclaim.

Above you see how Paul has combined Deuteronomy 9 and Deuteronomy 30 to make his own synthesis of the two. Deuteronomy 9 is a rebuke of thinking God chose Israel because of their own righteousness, and Deuteronomy 30 is an exhortation to remember that it was God who condescended and revealed His law rather than it being attained through great and laborious efforts. The Jewish people did not have to achieve or accomplish some difficult task; they did not have to raise themselves up to Heaven, nor even cross the oceans to find it. God supplied it, made it easy and simple. It did not depend on their own doing. Paul picks up these themes in Romans 10, describing the error of his Jewish opponents in terms of them seeking to establish their own righteousness, and contrasting the impossible way of doing with the easy way of believing. To insist upon your own doing is to deny the doing of Christ. To try to save yourself is to deny that Christ saves you. You do not ascend yourself to Heaven, as if Christ did not go there for you; you do not go down and raise yourself from the dead, as if Christ did not already descend for you. You do not 'do': you believe.

The righteousness of faith looks away from personal righteousness as a source of attaining blessing. It does not depend on going far away, up into heaven, or across and down into the deep, to procure for oneself salvation. Such attempts at saving oneself are a denial of the fact that it is God who mercifully and graciously condescends down to us, in our unrighteousness, and provides for us what we need, rather than we who somehow achieve or attain it by our own 'doings.' The righteousness of faith, in contrast to the righteousness of the law and the way of doing, is easy, near us, on our lips, and in our heart: *"If you declare with your mouth, 'Jesus is Lord,' and believe in your heart that God raised him from the dead, you will be saved" (10:9).*

In Chapter 11 Paul tells us that grace and works are incompatible as means of receiving election. *"If by grace, then it cannot be based on works; if it were, grace would no longer be grace" (11:6).* The contrast between grace and works makes very little sense if Paul is merely saying that Christians are supposed to replace an old set of rules with a new one. It makes perfect sense, however, indeed the etymology of the grace/works contrast is already explicit and clear, if what Paul is talking about is the difference between a gift you did not work for and a wage that you earned. And we know that is precisely what he is talking about, because he says so himself earlier in the same book: *"Now to the one who works, wages are not credited as a gift but as an obligation. However, to the one who does not work but trusts God who justifies the ungodly, their faith is credited as righteousness" (4:4-5).* Whether we think any Jews were guilty of trying to earn salvation, we cannot side-step the fact Paul preaches against it. Even if one wants to explain away every other passage, the language here is plain. Justification according to the law of works would enable one to boast, because workers earn a wage, and therefore recompense for them is what they deserve. But the ungodly sinner who simply trusts in the merciful God, is thereby given justification freely, despite not having worked for it or earned it, and it is this - the law of faith - which excludes boasting.

One last suggestion before we recap and close this defense of the Old Perspective: I would invite you to pick up the texts of Paul and read them a few times over, but each time with a different interpretive lens on. The first lens is a basically New Perspective lens. Try to read everything Paul says about works, justification, righteousness, the law, boasting, etc., simply in terms of a Jewish insistence on Judaism and the Jewish law, conflicts with Gentiles about ethnic privilege, and things of that sort. Any time a text seems to be saying something about trusting good works, self-righteousness, earning salvation, etc., try to see if you can make the text simply about the question of ethnicity, Judaism, and the relevance of the Mosaic law. If you have never read Paul this way, you might be surprised at how illuminating it is. A low Church evangelical who has only ever read Paul in terms of *sola fide* and earning salvation may, upon seeing these things in Paul for the first time, be very eager to dismiss the old perspective and run in haste to the revelatory power of the new. Paul certainly is talking about the issue of the Judaizers and the Mosaic law! But you will also find, at least eventually and after the novelty wears off, that reading Paul exclusively that way, with exclusively those lenses, poses its own difficulties. That in some texts it is very difficult, virtually impossible, to completely get rid of concepts like self-righteousness and trying to earn salvation. But now I ask you to remove those lenses, and go ahead and read through Paul again, but this time put on the lens of the Old Perspective. With this lens you are allowed to see all those questions about Judaism, the Mosaic Law, the Gentiles, ethnic divisions, etc., but where the text plainly contrasts earning salvation with receiving a free gift, plainly condemns self-righteous pride, etc., you're allowed to see it for what it plainly is. No twisting or forcing the text to say something else. This lens just works much better for the entirety of the text.

In addition, I want you to pay special attention to the arguments Paul makes about the works of the law. For example, *"For by the works of the law no human being will be justified in his sight, since through the law comes knowledge of sin"* *(Rom. 3:20)*. If we took this statement out of context, and substituted the words "commands of Christ" for the works of the law, would the argument still work? "Through the commands of Christ comes the knowledge of sin." It works perfectly - the commands of Christ actually reveal our sin *even more* than the Mosaic Law does:

> You have heard that the ancients were told, "You shall not murder," and "Whoever commits murder shall be answerable to the court." But I say to you that everyone who is angry with his brother shall be answerable to the court; and whoever says to his brother, "You good-for-nothing," shall be answerable to the supreme court; and whoever says, "You fool," shall be guilty enough to go into the fiery hell... You have heard that it was said, "You shall not commit adultery;" but I say to you that everyone who looks at a woman with lust for her has already committed adultery with her in his heart. (Matt. 5:21-22, 27-28)

The old law commanded us not to murder and not to commit adultery. Christ commands not to even think about it, not even a little bit. The commands of Christ reveals sin more truly and more deeply than the commands of Moses did. Hence many of Paul's arguments about the works of the law apply all the same to the commands of Christ - nay, they apply even more so. Is this a mere coincidence? Or could it be the case that Paul was not, in these instances, arguing against works qua the Mosaic law, but works qua works, works qua divine commands in general? When we step back and look at the broader sweep of his arguments, the etymology of his antithesis between grace and works, his explicit statements about works being "anything good or bad" (before you were even born) (Romans 9), his identification of the law with the general prohibition against sin (summed up as "do not covet") (Romans 7), his contrast between earning a wage and being justified as a gift you didn't work for (Romans 4), it becomes very hard to deny that Paul is, at least in some places, talking about these fundamental anthropological Old Perspective issues, and not just the question of Jewish ethnicity and an outdated law.

The response of those who have embraced the New Perspective will be confusion: "Sure, the 'old' lens makes it easy to understand the passages that seem to condemn earning salvation, but it's historically untenable that Paul was talking about that. Jews simply were not trying to earn salvation." Or perhaps someone might say, "Yes, it looks like Paul is talking about good works, but elsewhere Scripture is explicit that good works are required, so Paul simply cannot be talking about that."[47] The great Pauline scholar NT Wright, himself one of the most influential promoters of the New Perspective, admitted as much in his book, *Justification*, written in response to John Piper on this very issue.[48] The opening chapter contains a story about a good intentioned but

---

[47] The second objection, about the necessity of good works, will be answered in the climactic chapter of this book. But here I want to make a brief note about how we should read Paul. For another objection may arise when one is trying to make sense of his varied arguments, that the arguments themselves do not actually seem to prove the points he is making. For example, he questions whether the Galatians received the Spirit by faith or works, and implies this means works are not necessary. But one immediately notices when they put this into a syllogism, that the consequent does not follow. Many of his arguments, in fact, when formulated as syllogisms, do not work. At least, not without implicit premises, and, to use some Catholic ideas here, the allowance that he be arguing more from "fit" than strict logical necessity. Paul was not a logician, but a mystic. His arguments are not based on Aristotle but on allegory and experience. Not a systematic theologian - though he does offer theological treatise - but a biblical exegete and saint.

[48] While Wright has been a popularizer of the New Perspective, and is often arguing against the Old Perspective, he himself is not so easy to categorize, and probably should not be lumped into the New Perspective category, as at times he can say things that give credence to the Old, and to that extent, probably could be more

simple minded man who hears that people think the earth revolves around the sun, and perplexed by this, brings his friend outside one morning to watch the sunrise, proving that the sun clearly moves around the earth. Wright says this is what he feels like when explaining the New Perspective to men like Piper. He admits it seems like Paul is talking about 'Old Perspective' issues, just like it appears the sun moves around the earth. Of course, Wright wants us to accept that this is just the appearance, and what is actually going on under the surface of Paul is quite different. But the motivation for dismissing the appearance is the presupposition that Jewish people just simply were not trying to earn salvation. But we have already seen why this is false and how it fails to capture the history of the Jewish people and the problems that Jesus encountered and Paul addressed in their ministries. E.P. Sanders himself showed us that the Jewish people thought they merited their election by being more righteous than the nations. Like all humans of every age, the Jewish people indeed struggled with the temptation to attribute grace and blessings to their own deservedness, to their own righteousness. Throughout the Old Testament God is always reminding us that victory does not come by our own strength or achievements, but by His Spirit. And Jesus our Lord confronts, not just ethnic pride among the Jews, but also (even primarily) self-righteous pride and trusting in our own good works, too. His only parable explicitly about justification is couched in Pauline terms: the pious Pharisee, who trusts in his own works, and looks down upon others while merely paying lip service to grace, and the humble sinner who merely trusts God and entreats the divine mercy. Of these two, only one goes home "justified." Trusting one's good works was a problem that God saw fit to address in the New Testament, and He Himself addressed that problem by contrasting proud self-trust with humble trust in God. Only one of those sent a person home justified, only one attained the law they sought.

This sets the stage for what we read about in Paul. Of course, the crisis into which Paul wrote Galatians was not, explicitly at least, "people being taught they must earn salvation." No, the problem was that Christians were being told they must obey the Mosaic Law. But this fact about the Judaizers is taken as a sort of lynchpin that proves Paul was not also talking about good works, self-righteousness, and earning salvation. But what does Paul actually

---

readily fit into it. He can be tough to pin down, an Anglican who speaks in tongues, a conservative yet affirms female clergy, and seeming contradictions of these sorts. But that quite endears him to us, even if we do not always agree. He is a theologian of dialectic, who can say, "this, not that - well yes obviously that, but also not that in some important ways, and very much more so this."

say in response to those who insist that Christian righteousness depends on doing the law? His argument is not simply "the old law is no longer binding." He does make that point. There are times when the reason why works of the law do not justify is because they are works of an outdated law that was never intended to justify in the first place. But there are other times when the works of the law are addressed in terms equally applicable to divine law in general: The law reveals sin, no one has fulfilled the law, everyone has sinned, the commands themselves cannot give life, etc. This is all true of the Mosaic law, but they are also true of the commands of Christ. Is this a mere coincidence? Many of Paul's arguments against works of the law - especially the arguments in Romans - are made in such a way that they are equally applicable to divine law, and not just to the Mosaic law. This indicates Paul has shifted the discussion, broadened it, and is addressing the question of the Mosaic law by addressing the question of divine law in general. If good works cannot justify, then certainly circumcision cannot either.

The Gospel of salvation apart from all works is the answer to the question of Gentile inclusion apart from Torah works: i.e., if good works don't save, then certainly works of the old law don't either. Paul is addressing both of these, because both of these are going on in the background. On the one hand, there is confusion amongst Christians of goodwill about the relevance of the Mosaic law, whether they should be attempting to observe it or not. To these people he points out that the law was only meant to be temporary. It is fulfilled and outdated now in Christ. On the other hand, there is a vicious self-righteous pride involved in much of the Jewish insistence upon those works, and to those people, he points out that they are sinners too, and do not deserve, and cannot earn, by any works, their salvation. They can only receive it though humility, grace, and faith, as equals with Gentiles. These two problems are both being addressed, and Paul intertwines his arguments against both problems into one flowing discussion about the law, works, grace, and faith, in the context of the turn of salvation-history and in light of the cross of Christ. A difficulty people face when reading Paul is the way he goes back and forth between these different topics. Understanding that he is, in fact, going back and forth between them, is vital to understanding what he is saying, how he is intertwining and going back and forth between them.

In defending the Old Perspective on Paul, the goal here is not to say that in every passage which speaks of faith and works the primary target is always earning salvation. The first target, perhaps the primary target, is Gentile inclusion and the Mosaic Law. If someone has only heard *sola fide* preaching on Paul, they would do very well to pick up some New Perspective scholars (even perhaps some "Paul Within Judaism" scholars) and consider what they have to say. The salvation-historical questions that dominate the ministry of the apostle are key to understanding everything that was going on in the New Testament, and to understanding Paul's arguments and his response to the question of the Judaizers. But it was answering this question about the turn of salvation history that gave Paul the opportunity to expand on his insights into grace, faith, human sin and inability, and the free gift of God in Christ. The question he is answering is how the sinful, unworthy, unholy Gentiles, could be incorporated into the holy family of God. The answer is by faith, not by works and merits, but by the free grace of God won for us in Christ. He moves from the particular question to the universal answer, from a particular plight to the universal solution. The Jewish people had wrongly conceived of their election, an election they indeed knew was a gift of God, but a gift they believed they had earned by their righteous actions and by being more worthy than other peoples. The Pharisees had taught, at least by their actions, to look down upon the Gentile sinners, thinking themselves morally superior; and when they prayed and gave thanks to God, they were merely paying lip service to grace, while really trusting in their own piety… as if tithing of their dill and mint made up for a lack of justice, mercy, and faithfulness. The doctrine of justification answers the question of Gentile inclusion, cutting away all boasting, because you too, proud Pharisee, are a sinner too. The particular question of Jews, Gentiles, and the Mosaic law, is answered by the universal Gospel, that all people come together in Christ through faith, and not through works of (any) law.

Chapter 4
Faith and Works in the Rest of the Bible

**If you obey my commandments, you shall have life.
But if you disobey, all these curses will come upon you.
(Deut. 28:1-2, 15)**

It must be said from the outset that however clear we might find Paul about *sola fide*, the teaching is really found in only a few texts, and primarily just in Romans. Though there is plenty of material throughout Scripture which implicitly buttresses the doctrine, the texts which set salvation by faith in opposition to human "doing" are far outweighed by the overwhelming number of texts which starkly portray salvation as determined precisely by what we 'do.' There is a judgment, and God will not spare the wicked. Only those who obey will be saved (Isa. 1:28, Matt. 7:21, etc.). If all we had was the Old Testament, the fact that God's judgment is determined by what we do - by our works - would be virtually without doubt. Not that there aren't texts there which teach that righteous people must depend on mercy, grace, and the forgiveness of sins; but the picture painted is that God judges humanity on the basis of what we have done. From Ezekiel 18:

> The one who sins is the one who will die. Suppose there is a righteous man who does what is just and right...He follows my decrees and faithfully keeps my laws. That man is righteous; he will surely live, declares the Sovereign Lord. Suppose he has a violent son, who sheds blood or does any of these other things. He defiles his neighbor's wife. He oppresses the poor and needy. He commits robbery...Will such a man live? He will not! Because he has done all these detestable things, he is to be put to death; his blood will be on his own head.

People who sin will be condemned, even if they did good prior. But people who obey will be saved, even if they did wicked prior. Judgment, therefore, is based on what we do. There is forgiveness for those who repent, but the consistent theme throughout the entire Bible is that sinners and wicked people will be condemned while the righteous who obey the Lord will be saved.

The requirements for salvation boil down to one thing (i.e., a "yes" to God), but that one thing has several constitutive elements, and for the rest of this chapter we will work through the material in the New Testament collecting and assembling all those elements together. We will see that God has promised the gift of salvation only to those who persevere in repentant faith, and the existence of that promise is what makes meriting the gift of salvation possible.

Fiduciary Faith

The first aspect of New Testament teaching on salvation is faith. When asked what works they needed to do, our Lord told inquirers: *"This is the work of God, that you believe in Him whom He has sent"* (John 6:29). But the faith required is not a mental assent about Christ's existence. It is not merely knowing the truth. If faith is to have saving power, it must trust and expect His promises to come to pass. The biblical precedent is Abraham, who *"believed God, and this was credited to him as righteousness."* What Abraham believed was God's promise that he would become *"the father of many nations"* - and this, despite being nearly 100 years old. Abraham trusted that God would make him a father despite the biological evidence to the contrary. As an old man, he *"hoped against hope,"* expecting and believing that God would give him descendants as numerous as the stars. The faith that saves is a complete trusting of God, an entrusting of your entire life over to His care; it is a fiduciary faith that believes and trusts and expects the promises of God to come to pass, even when all the evidence is contrary - even when the world is falling down around us. If God says a flood is coming, we build an ark as our neighbors mock us. If Christ promises to resurrect us, we believe He will resurrect us even though we've never seen someone rise from the dead. *"For without faith it is impossible to please Him, for whoever would draw near to God must believe that he exists and that he rewards those who seek him"* (Heb. 11:6). Without faith salvation is impossible, and the faith that saves is a fiduciary faith that trusts in and expects God's promised reward.

Repentance

Faith is necessary, but repentance is also. Scripture is overwhelming here - apart from repentance the Christian cannot be saved. In point of fact, the predominant teaching of Jesus is that we need to be good people, and nearly everything he preaches centers on being and doing good as the path to Heaven:

> Blessed are the poor in spirit, for theirs is the kingdom of heaven. Blessed are those who mourn, for they will be

comforted. Blessed are the meek, for they will inherit the earth. Blessed are those who hunger and thirst for righteousness, for they will be filled. Blessed are the merciful, for they will be shown mercy. Blessed are the pure in heart, for they will see God. Blessed are the peacemakers, for they will be called children of God. Blessed are those who are persecuted because of righteousness, for theirs is the kingdom of heaven.

The good will be granted the kingdom of Heaven. Conversely, our Lord is adamant that those who do not practice His commands will not be saved: *"Those who do not obey the Son will not have life and will face God's wrath" (John 3:36).* What we do - whether good or bad - is undeniably determinative of our salvation. The heart of our Lord's teaching, the Sermon on the Mount, is dominated by this theme (Matt. 5:21-30):

You have heard that it was said to those of old, "You shall not murder; and whoever murders will be liable to judgment." But I say to you that everyone who is angry with his brother without cause will be liable to judgment; whoever insults his brother will be liable to the council; and whoever says, "You fool!" will be liable to the hell of fire. So if you are offering your gift at the altar and there remember that your brother has something against you, leave your gift there before the altar and go. First be reconciled to your brother, and then come and offer your gift. Come to terms quickly with your accuser while you are going with him to court, lest your accuser hand you over to the judge, and the judge to the guard, and you be put in prison. Truly, I say to you, you will not get out until you have paid the last penny.

You have heard that it was said, "You shall not commit adultery." But I say to you that everyone who looks at a woman with lust has already committed adultery with her in his heart. If your right eye causes you to sin, tear it out and throw it away. For it is better that you lose one of your members than that your whole body be thrown into hell. And if your right hand causes you to sin, cut it off and throw it away. For it is better that you lose one of your members than that your whole body go into hell.

Passages like these can be frightening, leaving no doubt we need to repent and live in accord with God's will to be saved. Our being forgiven is contingent upon us forgiving others (Matt. 6:14-15), and we will be judged the way we judge others (Matt. 7:1-2). Our hearts cannot be right with God unless they are right with those around us. We might know and trust the truth about Jesus, but if we deny him in front of others, He will deny us in front of the Father (Matt. 10:32-33). We might even have some sort of love for Christ, but if we love the things of this world more than we love Him, we are not worthy of Him (Matt. 10:37). Only those who lose their life for His sake will find it (Matt. 10:39). If we start behaving wickedly while waiting for His return, He will return when we do not expect, and will assign us a place *"where there will be weeping and gnashing of teeth" (Matt. 24:45-51)*. Those who fail to help the poor will be guilty of failing to help our Lord, and will be cast into the *"eternal fire prepared for the devil" (Matt. 25:41-45)*:

> Then he will say to those on his left, "Depart from me, you who are cursed, into the eternal fire prepared for the devil and his angels. For I was hungry and you gave me nothing to eat, I was thirsty and you gave me nothing to drink, I was a stranger and you did not invite me in, I needed clothes and you did not clothe me, I was sick and in prison and you did not care for me."

> They also will answer, "Lord, when did we see you hungry or thirsty or a stranger or needing clothes or sick or in prison, and did not help you?"

> He will reply, "Truly I tell you, whatever you did not do for one of the least of these, you did not do for me."

What we do determines our salvation. Did we care for the poor or ignore them? Did we forgive others or condemn them? We are only God's friends if we do what He commands (John 15:14). There is no question, in the teaching of Christ, repentance is absolutely necessary for salvation. Even Paul, our beloved teacher of *sola fide*, says the same thing. Paul repeatedly warns us: do not be deceived: people who do not repent - people who live a wicked and sinful life - such people will not be saved:

> Or do you not know that evildoers will not inherit the kingdom of God? Do not be deceived: Neither the sexually immoral, nor idolaters, nor adulterers, nor men who have sex with men, nor thieves, nor the greedy, nor drunkards, nor slanderers, nor swindlers, will inherit the kingdom of God. (1 Cor. 6:9-10)

> The acts of the flesh are obvious: sexual immorality, impurity and debauchery; idolatry and witchcraft; malice, discord, jealousy, fits of rage, selfish ambition, dissensions, factions and envy; drunkenness, orgies, and the like. I warn you, as I did before, that those who live like this will not inherit the kingdom of God. (Gal. 5:19-21)

> But among you there must not be a hint of sexual immorality, or of any kind of impurity, or of greed, because these are improper for God's holy people. Nor should there be obscenity, foolish talk or coarse joking, which are out of place, but rather thanksgiving. For of this you can be sure: No immoral, impure or greedy person—such a person is an idolater—has any inheritance in the kingdom of Christ and of God. (Eph. 5:3-5)

These testimonies are repetitious and explicit. Any doctrine of justification by faith must be tempered and balanced by an insistence on repentance. But this brings an objection: does not faith guarantee repentance? Is it not true that good works are the fruit of saving faith and impossible unless one is already saved? That we do good because we have been saved and not in order to be? There is some truth there, depending on the way we define our terms. But basic faith, just simply knowing and believing that Jesus Christ is the incarnate Son of God, that He died for your sins and rose again, does not automatically guarantee repentance. Our Lord indicates this in Matthew 7 among other places,

> Not everyone who says to me, "Lord, Lord," will enter the kingdom of heaven, but only the one who does the will of my Father who is in heaven. Many will say to me on that day, "Lord, Lord, did we not prophesy in your name and in your name drive out demons and in your name perform many miracles?" Then I will tell them plainly, "I never knew you. Away from me, evildoers!"

These people are condemned despite not only believing in Jesus, but even doing miracles in His name. They knew as clearly as anyone knows that Jesus is Lord. Why then were they condemned? They were evildoers. They did not repent. The Epistle of James is equally forceful about the fruitlessness of bare faith sans repentance:

> You believe God is one. You do well; the demons also believe, and shudder. But are you willing to acknowledge, you foolish person, that faith without works is useless?...You see that a person is justified by works and not by faith alone. (Jas. 2:19-20, 24)

There is nothing about faith which automatically guarantees a person will repent. This cuts against the grain of certain Protestant theologies which claim that true faith always produces good fruits, and against the claim that if a person isn't doing good then it means they don't truly believe. This was one of Luther's errors - he claimed it was impossible for a person to lead a life of wanton sin while trusting in the promises of Christ. But his position can only come from inexperience with sin and a naivety about the ability of people to say to themselves, "Christ is so good and merciful, He will surely save me - He died to save me" and then use that truth as justification to go on sinning all they want. In the midst of the most wicked of lifestyles, people can still trust in Christ and be (wrongly) confident of their salvation. But we have seen from Scripture how preposterous it is to think a person would be saved in the midst of such a lifestyle without repenting. Despite their faith and trust in Christ, if they do not repent, and persist in sin, they will only hear, "You believe? So do the demons. Now away from me, evildoers."

None of this means, however, that a person should trust in anything other than the Cross of Christ. It may be possible to be damned for impenitence despite trusting the Cross, but an equally paved highway to hell is trusting your own works rather than in God. Repentance needs to repent of self-trust just as much as it needs to repent of every other form of carnality. Self-righteousness is as sure a ticket to condemnation as adultery. Paul warns of this throughout his epistles (as does our Lord in his parables): those who seek justification by the law, who seek to stand before God on the basis of their own performance and merits, will by that effort sever themselves from Christ:

> Mark my words! I, Paul, tell you that if you let yourselves be circumcised, Christ will be of no value to you. Again I declare to everyone who lets himself be circumcised that he is

obligated to obey the whole law. You who are trying to be justified by the law have been cut off from Christ; you have fallen away from grace. (Gal. 5:2-4)

Perseverance

The end of the previous section segways perfectly to the next. In addition to repenting, a person must persevere in their repentance. Salvation is not a one-time event, in which the finish is guaranteed from the start. There is a race we must run, a struggle to remain in the faith until the end. In the passage at the end of the previous section, the Galatians were warned about seeking justification by the law. Going that route would result in them being *"cut off from Christ"* and *"fallen from grace."* The Galatians were already justified, had already received the indwelling Holy Spirit (Gal. 3:2-3). Paul's warning to them was that, if, after already being justified, they were then to seek justification by the law, they would fall from grace. Christ would be of no more benefit to them. They would be severed from Christ whom they had previously been united to. They would forfeit their justification. Salvation thus depends on our perseverance in the faith. Falling from, abandoning, forfeiting… "losing" salvation is a possibility. Our Lord says, *"the one who stands firm to the end will be saved" (Matt. 10:22).* This endurance is not guaranteed to all who are born-again by the Spirit. In a parable about new life in Christ, our Lord speaks of some people who immediately sprout up, but afterwards, in times of testing, fall away:

> Then he told them many things in parables, saying: "A farmer went out to sow his seed. As he was scattering the seed, some fell along the path, and the birds came and ate it up. Some fell on rocky ground, where it did not have much soil. It sprang up quickly because the soil was shallow. But when the sun came up, the plants were scorched, and they withered because they had no root. Other seed fell among thorns, which grew up and choked the plants. Still other seed fell on good soil, where it produced a crop—a hundred, sixty or thirty times what was sown."
>
> "Listen then to what the parable of the sower means: When anyone hears the message about the kingdom and does not understand it, the evil one comes and snatches away what was sown in their heart. This is the seed sown along the path. The seed falling on rocky ground refers to someone who hears the word and receives it with joy. But since they have no root,

they last only a short time. When trouble or persecution comes because of the word, they quickly fall away. The seed falling among the thorns refers to someone who hears the word, but the worries of this life and the deceitfulness of wealth choke the word, making it unfruitful. But the seed falling on good soil refers to someone who hears the word and understands it. This is the one who produces a crop, yielding a hundred, sixty or thirty times what was sown." (Matt. 13:3-8, 18-23)

Salvation can be squandered. If after we've been forgiven, we turn around and act unmercifully to others, God will rescind the mercy previously given to us (Matt. 18:32-35). The Lord gives believers talents of gold, but if he returns and finds we have done nothing with them, he will throw us *"into outer darkness"* (Matt. 25:24-30). Like a gardener, the Father prunes those branches in Him that do not bear fruit (John 15:1-6):

I am the true vine, and my Father is the gardener. He cuts off every branch in me that bears no fruit, while every branch that does bear fruit he prunes so that it will be even more fruitful. You are already clean because of the word I have spoken to you. Remain in me, as I remain in you. No branch can bear fruit by itself; it must remain in the vine. Neither can you bear fruit unless you remain in me. I am the vine; you are the branches. If you remain in me and I in you, you will bear much fruit; apart from me you can do nothing. If you do not remain in me, you are like a branch that is thrown away and withers; such branches are picked up, thrown into the fire and burned.

The apostle Paul picks up this same agricultural metaphor to describe the way Gentiles have been grafted into the people of God, warning that those who do not continue in the faith will be cut off from the branch:

They were broken off because of unbelief, and you stand by faith. Do not be arrogant, but tremble. For if God did not spare the natural branches, he will not spare you either. Consider therefore the kindness and sternness of God: sternness to those who fell, but kindness to you, provided that you continue in his kindness. Otherwise, you too will be cut off. (Rom. 11:20-22)

Paul repeats this warning about the necessity of perseverance throughout his letters. In Cor. 15:2, *"By this gospel you are saved, if you hold firmly to the word I preached to you. Otherwise, you have believed in vain;"* and Col. 1:22, *"But now he has reconciled you…if you continue in your faith, established and firm, and do not move from the hope held out in the gospel."* The final salvation of the Christian is not guaranteed the moment they are justified. The apostle John knew there was a possibility of turning around and forfeiting salvation, and wrote to admonish Christians so that they would not: *"All this I have told you so that you will not fall away" (1 John 16:1).* Peter writes about those who, after being once saved, turn back to their previous life of sin:

> For if, after they have escaped the defilements of the world by the knowledge of the Lord and Savior Jesus Christ, they are again entangled in them and are overcome, the last state is worse for them than the first. For it would be better for them not to have known the way of righteousness, than having known it, to turn away from the holy commandment handed on to them. (2 Pet. 2:20-21)

Initial justification does not guarantee final salvation, but rather, and frighteningly so, makes any eventual return to impenitence all the more twisted and damning (*"the last state has become worse for them than the first"*). Our Lord speaks about this terrible state of affairs that comes about when a person is cleaned but then returns to their former life in Matt. 12:43-45,

> When an evil spirit comes out of a person, it goes through dry places seeking rest but does not find it. Then it says, "I will return to the house I left." When it arrives, it finds the house unoccupied, swept clean and put in order. Then it goes and takes with it seven other spirits more wicked than itself, and they go in and live there. And the final condition of that person is worse than the first.

Perhaps the most frightening of all the passages on the possibility of turning around and falling away from salvation are found in the Book of Hebrews. The clear and emphatic warnings in that book speak for themselves:

> See to it, brothers and sisters, that none of you has a sinful, unbelieving heart that turns away from the living God. But encourage one another daily, as long as it is called "Today," so that none of you may be hardened by sin's deceitfulness. We have come to share in Christ, if indeed we maintain our initial conviction until the end. (Heb. 3:12-14)

> It is impossible for those who have been enlightened, who have tasted the heavenly gift, who have shared in the Holy Spirit, who have tasted the goodness of the word of God and the powers of the coming age, and who have then fallen away, to be brought back to repentance. To their loss they are crucifying the Son of God all over again and subjecting him to public disgrace. (Heb. 6:4-6)

> If we deliberately keep on sinning after we have received the knowledge of the truth, no sacrifice for sins remains, but only a fearful expectation of judgment and fire that consumes the enemies of God. (Heb. 10:26-27)

In light of our need to maintain repentance in a world filled with temptation and trial - and the looming possibility of damnation if we do not - Paul exhorts Christians to *"work out your salvation with fear and trembling" (Phil. 2:12)*. There is a race we need to run, a fight we need to fight. Even though Paul was the recipient of unspeakable graces, without a doubt standing in the most profound of blessings, he disciplined himself so as to not be disqualified, striving to win the crown God has promised those who finish the race. From 1 Cor. 9:24-27:

> Do you not know that the runners in the stadium all run in the race, but there is only one who wins the prize? Run so as to win. Every athlete exercises discipline to win a perishable crown, but we an imperishable one. Thus I do not run aimlessly; I do not fight as if I were shadowboxing. No, I discipline my body and train it, for fear that, after having preached to others, I myself should be disqualified.

Salvation is presented as a prize that we can win by finishing the race. But we must run according to the rules. A runner who starts well can be disqualified if they stray from the path. But God promises the reward to all who keep the faith until the end:

> I have fought the good fight, I have finished the race, I have kept the faith. Now there is in store for me the crown of righteousness, which the Lord, the righteous Judge, will award to me on that day—and not only to me, but all who have longed for his coming. (2 Tim. 4:7-8)

Merit

The nature of salvation as something that God has promised as a reward creates the possibility of merit. Since God has promised salvation to those who finish the face, those who finish the race merit what God has promised. But didn't Paul say that salvation is not something we merit? In Romans 4 he says this, *"to the one who works his wages (μισθός/misthos) are not a gift but what he has merited."* There is a sense in which we cannot merit salvation. Everyone has sinned and deserves condemnation. Also, salvation is supernatural and thus outside of human power to attain. There is nothing we can do to achieve it for ourselves. But God, in His mercy and grace, condescends to us, dies for our sins, and through His atoning blood, makes salvation open to us; and in His grace, lifts up our dead and wicked hearts so that we desire His gift, and enables us and works in us to bring us to faith and repentance. All of this is a grace that we do not deserve and cannot merit. Neither could we merit the promise of salvation for those who finish the race. But once the promise, which we could not merit, has been made, we can then merit what has been promised. So, while we cannot merit the "wage" of salvation, there is another sense in which we can: because God has promised to save those who repent, therefore, those who repent merit what God has promised. All throughout the preaching of our Lord, salvation is presented as a reward we can merit by doing the will of God. Pay attention to the Greek word here in these passages (μισθός/misthos). This is the same word from Romans 4 mentioned earlier in this paragraph.

> Blessed are you when people insult you, persecute you, and falsely say all kinds of evil against you because of me. Rejoice and be glad, because great is your reward (μισθός/misthos) in heaven, for in the same way they persecuted the prophets before you. (Matt. 5:11)

> When you give to the needy, do not let your left hand know what your right is doing, so that your giving may be in secret. Then your Father, who sees what is done in secret, will reward (μισθός/misthos) you…when you pray, go into your room, close the door and pray to your Father, who is unseen. Then your Father, who sees what is done in secret, will reward (μισθός/misthos) you. (Matt. 6:1-6)

> Anyone who welcomes you welcomes me, and anyone who welcomes me welcomes the One who sent me. Whoever welcomes a prophet as a prophet will receive a prophet's

> reward (μισθς/misthos), and whoever welcomes a righteous person will receive a righteous person's reward (μισθς/misthos). And if anyone gives a cup of cold water to one of these little ones who is my disciple, truly I tell you, that person will certainly not lose their reward (μισθς/misthos). (Matt. 10:40-42)

The ability to merit salvation is further supported by another parable in which salvation is explicitly likened to a wage earned by employees. The point of the parable is to undercut any pride and bitterness that might develop in the hearts of those who resent God's mercy, but it nevertheless portrays believers as hired employees who earn the wage of salvation by working for God:

> For the kingdom of heaven is like a landowner who went out early in the morning to hire workers for his vineyard. He agreed to pay them a denarius for the day and sent them into his vineyard....

> When evening came, the owner of the vineyard said to his foreman, "Call the workers and pay them their wages (μισθς/misthos), beginning with the last ones hired and going on to the first."

> The workers who were hired about five in the afternoon came and each received a denarius. So those who were hired first expected to receive more. But each one of them also received a denarius...

> So the last will be first, and the first will be last. (Matt. 20: 1-2, 8-10, 16)

This "leveling of the playing field" between those who labor for God for many years and those who receive death-bed mercy does not eliminate the ability to merit salvation. Rather, it is predicated on the ability for everyone, even those in their dying moments, to do so. Everyone who works for the Lord earns the wage, whether they work but a single hour or a whole day. Those who do the will of God draw a wage for doing so:

> Even now the one who reaps draws a wage (μισθς/misthos) and harvests a crop for eternal life, so that the sower and the reaper may be glad together. Thus the saying "One sows and another reaps" is true. I sent you to reap what you have not worked for. Others have done the work, and you have reaped the benefits of their labor. (John 4:36-38)

Everyone merits what they sow, whether by doing evil they merit destruction, or by walking in the Spirit they merit eternal life: *"Whoever sows to their flesh, from the flesh will reap destruction; whoever sows to please the Spirit, from the Spirit will reap eternal life" (Gal. 6:8).*

The New Testament, as the whole of Scripture, informs us that salvation is something we must merit by repenting of sin, by fighting the good faith of faith, and finishing the race with repentance intact. There is a dialectic here, Romans 4: that salvation is not a *wage/μισθς/misthos;* and Matt. 5:11, 6:1-6, 10:40-42, 20: 1-16, and John 4:36-38: in which salvation is a *wage/μισθς/misthos.* There is a sense in which salvation is not a wage we merit, but there is another sense in which it is a wage we must. The reward of salvation isn't guaranteed by faith apart from repentance, nor does being born-again and transformed by the Spirit of God necessitate that we will continue on in that life of sanctification. Only by the grace of God, but by the grace of God, we must cooperate with God, turn from sin, do the work of repentance, and work out our salvation with fear and trembling. While 'outer darkness' and 'the fire that consumes the enemies of God' looms as a threat for those who turn away from grace, God promises to help us on our way, and if we abide in Him, we are promised the unfathomable reward of eternal life as recompense. Indeed, justifying faith requires that we believe God "rewards those who earnestly seek him" (Heb. 11:6). Our faith is not complete if we do not believe in some form of grace-based merit and rewards from God, given to those who seek Him - but neither is our faith complete, if we are trusting in our own works and merits, and not in the Lord. To the nature of this dialectic, we now turn.

Chapter 5
The Dialectic of Salvation

A Contradiction?

Throughout church history, the chorus of the greatest Catholic authorities, all interpreted Paul's doctrine of justification as excluding good works and earning salvation. There was a certain *sola fide* in their understanding of Paul. But at the dawn of the Reformation there was no Catholic dogma on the question of justification. There was a tradition, but various streams within it. You could find preaching with an emphasis on good works and the necessity of meriting salvation through ascetic practices. You could also find those voices which spoke about the free grace of God and the assurance of forgiveness in the shed blood of Christ, received through faith. Luther had been weighed down under a teaching, or least an understanding, that was more of the former. His superiors in the Augustinian order had pointed him to resources that spoke of grace, but Luther ultimately felt separation from the Church was the only way to affirm *sola fide* - or at least, to do so without fear of being killed. And it was true that persistence in affirming it, while trying to remain a faithful Catholic, would have likely led to his martyrdom. It was also true that it would have been impossible to remain Catholic while completely rejecting merit and works in every sense from salvation. But there was, and continues to be, a way to parse out the Catholic teaching with an emphasis on *sola fide* without also denying the validity of merit. And after the Reformation had been at work for some 20 odd years throughout Europe, the Church convened a Council to decide exactly how it would parse out the Catholic position.

Unfortunately, a tone of reconciliation with Protestants was not the course the Council would take. Instead of picking up the Dominican mantra, "never deny, seldom affirm, always make distinctions," the Council took a hostile approach. Condemnations of Protestant slogans were pronounced without semblance of nuance. The dogmas which came forth from the Council made for more heightened conflict with Protestant understandings than necessary. Three of them are particularly relevant for our discussion:

> If any one saith, that by faith alone the impious is justified...let him be anathema.

> If any one saith, that the (justification) received is not preserved and also increased before God through good works...let him be anathema.

> If any one saith, that the good works of one that is justified...does not truly merit increase of grace, eternal life, and the attainment of that eternal life...let him be anathema.

To the reader who was paying attention to the third chapter at what Catholics throughout history had said about justification, good works, and merit, it might seem that these canons had in effect anathematized a whole chorus of Saints and Doctors of the Church.

Here a pause is required to explain what we have been saying about tones of reconciliation and hostility, and ways of phrasing and parsing things out. We must be aware of the difference between words and concepts. How the Council of Trent phrased its teaching is one thing, the substance beneath those words is another. One can have orthodox substance despite difficult phrasing. For example, the phrase "God creates evil." Is this true? Well, if what you mean is that God brings disaster and condemnation upon the wicked, or that God brings good things out of the evil that creatures do, then the phrase is orthodox with regard to its substance, but the phrasing, the words used, are perhaps a bit problematic. God creates evil? As if God directly causes people to sin, or worse, does evil things Himself? The words used can lead to misunderstandings. Now imagine a student of theology using this phrase, "God creates evil," in one of their papers. The first professor to come across this sharply corrects the student, "This is incorrect. God does no such thing." But a second professor comes along, thinks upon the fact that this phrase can actually be found in the Bible (Is. 45:7), and explains to his student, "The bible does at times speak that way, and there is a sense in which it's true; but we must be careful in how we speak, for that phrase could be misleading. It is better to say that God does not do evil, but that He is in control of all things and sometimes uses natural disasters and various evils in order to accomplish His will providentially." This second professor, being a good Thomist, spoke with nuance and a tone of reconciliation. He did not deny (for no one is ever completely wrong), nor did he fully affirm (for rarely is anyone ever completely right), but he made the proper distinctions. Now the Council of Trent, in responding to Protestant teaching, could have taken this latter path, but instead, it took the hostile approach of the former. The Council wasn't wrong in its correction, it just could have been better; it could have been less concerned with condemning Protestants and more focused on unity and affirming what was good and true in Protestant thinking.

The Council declared three things which on the surface appear to be in direct opposition to Pauline teaching about justification: that justification is not by faith alone, that justification is preserved and increased by good works, and that the good works of the justified merit eternal life. In the eyes of many Protestant scholars today, the Council did not just superficially, linguistically contradict Paul, but did so actually, in substance. And many Catholics, zealous to defend the infallibility of the Council and its teachings on justification, respond by denying the antecedent. They assert that Protestants have just misunderstood Paul, and use the New Perspective reading as proof that Paul never ruled out good works or merits but only the works of the Jewish law. These Catholics often claim, like we saw at the beginning of the third chapter, that Catholics always understood the "works of the law" in Paul as denoting only the works of the Jewish law and not good works in general. By embracing this perspective on Paul, they think they have escaped the accusation made by Protestants that Catholic teaching contradicts scripture. For in the eyes of many, if the Old Perspective was right about Paul, there would be a contradiction between Church teaching (not by faith alone) and that of the Apostle (by faith alone).

What Trent Meant

The weight of explaining the Tridentine teaching bears down upon us. What exactly did it mean, we can merit salvation? Why aren't we justified by faith alone? How can good works "preserve and increase" our justification? Of preeminent importance here are definitions. Imagine that what Trent meant by the word "faith" was love for God - and then said humans cannot be saved by "love for God" alone? Or, if "justification" meant only "legal acquittal," how could a yes-or-no, on-or-off, guilty or not, category like that, possibly "increase"? A person is either condemned or acquitted. Your acquittal is either granted or it is not. Language of "increase" would be nonsensical if that's what "justification" meant. Perhaps the most troubling of the Tridentine language... if by "merit" the Church meant that a human being could save themselves? And be puffed up with pride and self-righteousness? If this was what Trent meant, the Protestant reaction would be more than understandable. It would be downright generous.

But let us discover what the Church actually meant, and we will quickly see that it is far from approaching the problematic definitions just suggested (or from anything that substantially, rather than merely linguistically, contradicts Paul). Beginning with the word faith, when Trent said that justification is not by "faith" alone, the definition of faith in operation is that of a purely intellectual assent - a pure "knowing" the truth about God and Christ, isolated from any form of repentance, cooperation with grace, or love for God. That this is the definition of faith being used is made clear by looking at the complete canon, which reads,

> If any one saith, that by faith alone the impious is justified; in such wise as to mean, that nothing else is required to co-operate in order to the obtaining the grace of Justification, and that it is not in any way necessary, that he be prepared and disposed by the movement of his own will; let him be anathema.

The Council is condemning a precise understanding of faith alone: only rejecting it if it is meant *"in such wise as to mean"* that faith is completely passive and involves no movement of the human will. The mention of "preparation for justification" refers back to earlier in the sixth session, where it is taught that justification occurs, apart from prior merits on our part, when the prevenient grace of God enables and moves us to repent of sin, to begin to hope in God and trust in His promises, and to approach baptism in faith to receive justifying grace:

> The beginning of the said Justification is to be derived from the prevenient grace of God, through Jesus Christ, that is to say, from His vocation, whereby, without any merits existing on their parts, they are called; that so they, who by sins were alienated from God, may be disposed through His quickening and assisting grace, to convert themselves to their own justification, by freely assenting to and co-operating with that said grace: in such sort that, while God touches the heart of man by the illumination of the Holy Ghost, neither is man himself utterly without doing anything while he receives that inspiration, forasmuch as he is also able to reject it; yet is he not able, by his own free will, without the grace of God, to move himself unto justice in His sight.

And

> Now they (adults) are disposed unto the said justice, when, excited and assisted by divine grace, conceiving faith by hearing, they are freely moved towards God, believing those things to be true which God has revealed and promised,-and this especially, that God justifies the impious by His grace,

through the redemption that is in Christ Jesus; and when, understanding themselves to be sinners, they, by turning themselves, from the fear of divine justice whereby they are profitably agitated, to consider the mercy of God, are raised unto hope, confiding that God will be propitious to them for Christ's sake; and they begin to love Him as the fountain of all justice; and are therefore moved against sins by a certain hatred and detestation, to wit, by that penitence which must be performed before baptism.

This "preparation" for justification, enabled and moved by grace, is thus not strictly monergistic, but depends in some part on the cooperation of our own will. While we do not have the free-will to repent and choose God on our own apart from grace, when grace comes, it (He) enables us to do so. This cooperation with God as He moves us to repentance is what the Council describes as our "preparation" for justification: repenting of sin and placing our trust in God. Apart from this cooperation (repentance) we cannot be saved. Thus, when the Council rejected justification by "faith" alone, it was rejecting the idea that mere mental assent possesses justifying power. It was not rejecting justification by repentance, but asserting the necessity of it.

A quick note before moving on. We just said that the Council of Trent defined faith in terms of mental assent. The Catholic tradition indeed speaks of three separate theological virtues: faith, hope, and love. They are distinct, and while love cannot exist without hope and faith, and hope cannot exist without faith, faith - being mental assent - can exist apart from hope and love. What this means is that a person can truly believe and know that Christ is their God and Savior, that He died for them and rose again, and yet, if they do not also, in addition to believing, repent of sin and receive from God hope and love, they do not therefore possess the fullness of justification. Furthermore, a person can truly trust in Christ alone for their salvation, and yet, despite trusting Him and His promises for their salvation, if they do not also repent of their sins, they therefore do not possess justification. Faith and trust alone, apart from repentance, does not save. This goes against the typical Protestant idea, expressed by Luther, that true faith always necessarily produces repentance and good works. Unless faith is defined as repentance and/or love for God, or unless the person adheres to a doctrine of infallible efficacious grace which guarantees the sanctification of all who have mere mental assent (which is clearly unscriptural, c.f. the "Lord, Lord" of Matt. 7:21), then it is untenable to think that faith automatically produces good works. In fact, far from faith guaranteeing repentance, an excess of trust in God's mercy is possible, such that you think, because God is merciful (indeed He died for you), it doesn't matter how much you sin, He will surely save you anyway. Evidently, faith and trust in God, when understood this way, isolated from repentance, does not save, nor does it guarantee that good works will follow. But, and this is of absolutely crucial importance for understanding justification and Paul and Church teaching, so pay extra attention here, if what is meant by faith is not just intellectual assent or trust alone, but that a person actually loves Christ, then this faith, which is really faith, hope, and love together, certainly possesses the full power of justification. More will be said about this later, but it suffices for now to explain what Trent meant, and did not mean, by rejecting justification by faith alone. Justification cannot be said to be 'by faith alone,' if it is said *"in such wise to mean"* that justification is by mental assent alone. But justification by *repentant* faith alone was not condemned.

Moving on, what does it mean that good works "preserve and increase justice"? Notice the word justice here - earlier we translated it as justification. Whenever we see the words, righteous, righteousness, justice, justified, justification, or any of these cognates in Scripture or theology, the root biblical word in the Greek New Testament is the same: δίκαιος, or, transliterated, dikaios. Its semantic range includes ideas like upright, righteous, virtuous, approved of (or) acceptable to God, rendering to each his due (and that in a judicial sense), passing just judgment on others, innocent, faultless, etc. Now when Protestants speak of justification, they have a narrow and specific definition in mind, and they are usually trying to stick very closely to the way they think Paul uses it in key texts like Romans 3-4. But when the Council of Trent defined it, it did not seek to define it only what Paul meant by his use of the term in those key texts. Rather, the Council defined the word in a broader sense, including the fuller breadth of the semantic range, denoting not only "being made right with God," but the entire category of righteousness before God. "Justification," then, in the Conciliar text, is not only being made righteous, but includes maintaining and growing in righteousness as well. More on this point will be said in the last chapter on Imputation, and later on this chapter when discussing whether *sola fide* is only applicable to initial justification.

Now in the previous chapter we noted that Augustine interpreted "justification" in the Pauline texts in terms of a foundational, basic, yes-or-no sense, of being made righteous before God, such that good works could not cause it, even beyond initial justification, but could only follow it and flow from it. And we agree that when Paul is using the term in key justification texts, he seems to be using it in that narrow sense. But in his general preaching Augustine can use the term in the more broadened Tridentine sense as well. See for example in *Sermon 158,*

> We have been justified; but this justice can grow, as we make progress. And how it can grow I will tell you, and after a fashion compare notes with you, so that you may all, each and every one of you, already established in the condition of justification, namely by receiving the forgiveness of sins in the washing of regeneration, by receiving the Holy Spirit, by making progress day by day; so that you may all see where you are, put your best foot forward, make progress and grow.

Now I share this passage from Augustine for a couple of reasons. First, the concept of "increasing justification" has, in the field of scholarship, even Catholic scholarship, been hitherto considered a linguistic innovation of the fathers at Trent. This text from Augustine shows they were actually using patristic phraseology. Second, the authority of Augustine is cherished by Protestants and perhaps his testimony on this point may provide additional credence to the Tridentine doctrine. Using the word 'justification' in a broadened sense to include not only the foundational, yes-or-no right standing with God, but the entire situation of human righteousness before God, something which can increase with good works, was a practice of Augustine, and not just a medieval Catholic development.

In the teaching of the Council of Trent, a person is initially made righteous when, at the point of their conversion, they have their sins forgiven and they receive justifying grace (i.e., love for God), from God. They are changed, converted, transformed from an unrighteous sinner into a righteous man. Apart from any merits or good works on their part, as a completely free gift of His mercy, God comes to the sinner, who previously was set on wickedness and had no care for God or doing His will. But the grace of God comes, works repentance into us, fills us with faith and love, and sets our will on doing His. Though we were ungodly, and could do nothing to save ourselves, God comes to us and makes us into a just person, by converting us and granting us repentance. He justifies us by His grace, apart from our works, through faith. After that initial conversion, the preservation of justification depends on the continued existence of repentant faith within us. If a person was to abandon repentance, turn to a willful embrace of sin, turn their backs on God, then they would no longer possess a disposition instrumental of sanctifying grace. They would no longer be just. By embracing deliberate and explicit sin, a person destroys their relationship with God, falls from grace, and severs themselves from Christ (Gal. 5:4). Therefore, all those behaviors involved with building us in our faith, resisting temptation, and avoiding an embrace of sin, all work to preserve repentance, and thereby preserve justification. Put simply, behaviors (works) that preserve repentance are behaviors that preserve justification. That is what Trent meant when it said good works preserve justification: doing things that help you keep the faith, is doing things that help you keep your justice. Paul alludes to this link between good works and perseverance when he says that he disciplined his body so that he would not be disqualified from salvation (*"I strictly discipline my body and make it my slave, so that, after I have preached to others, I myself will not be disqualified,"* 1 Cor. 9:27). He was aware of the potential to fall from grace, and he knew he could help ensure his continued relationship with God by doing works of renunciation, fasting, practicing the disciplines of prayer, etc.

Can we increase in our justification? Protestants of every tradition agree that we can grow in our personal sanctity and holiness, and this is all the Church means by speaking of behaviors, or works, which increase justification. It is not as if good works can bring a person into a right relationship with God. Good works are not possible unless you are first righteous, and justification occurs by grace through faith the moment we repent (quite apart from whether we have done any good works prior). But a person can, through good works, increase their closeness and intimacy with God. Good works can increase our holiness and sanctity and righteousness. This suffices for now, for more will be said on that point in the later section on initial justification and the last chapter on Imputation.

Merit

The doctrine of merit is often needlessly complicated by good intentioned Catholics.[49] They want to emphasize the Christological nature of

---

[49] I am reminded of a time when a Protestant seminary student, interested in Catholicism, asked me, a fellow student in the seminary and recent zealous convert to Catholicism, to explain the Catholic teaching on salvation. My understanding at that time was erroneous, complex, and ultimately, obfuscated the issue. I had heard apologists and scholars alike, both describing salvation as ontological, talking about sanctifying grace as a "physical accident" which God "infuses into the soul" - and because at that time I had a quasi-Cartesian dualistic anthropology that entailed a material soul inhabiting the physical body, I tried to explain to the poor girl how salvation meant the ontological substance of the soul glowed with supernatural radiance, that sin destroyed and darkened this substance, etc. Of course, that understanding is not entirely wrong, but it's just slightly wrong on some important

merit, and construe it in terms of an intrinsic value due to the works Christ Himself does in us. Now of course the works of Christ are meritorious, but merit accrues directly to the cooperative works of the Christian, and not to the gracious promptings of Christ within us. The existence of merit stems not so much from the supernatural quality of the works per se,[50] but from the simple fact that God has promised recompense to them. The existence of merit is this simple: God has promised eternal life to those who do His will, therefore, those who do His will merit eternal life.

Imagine I walk into a room and announce to everyone, "whoever goes across the street and brings me back a bottle of water, I will give one trillion dollars." The promised recompense far outweighs the intrinsic value of getting a bottle of water. In reality any human court would judge the promise invalid due to it being so outrageous that no reasonable person would think it serious. But imagine I had trillions of trillions of trillions of dollars to give, such that giving the money away would make me no less unfathomably rich. And imagine I was serious as death and taxes when I made the offer. Now if someone took me up on the offer and went across the street and brought me back a bottle of water, they would have every right to those trillion dollars. They did what was required, I made them a promise, so now I owe them it. Even though the action isn't intrinsically worth a trillion dollars, there is of course a sense in which they have, by doing it, merited that sum, simply because I made a serious and valid promise to pay it.

This is all, and this is precisely, what the term 'merit' means in Catholic teaching: because God has promised salvation to those who do God's will, therefore, those who do God's will, merit what God promised. It means nothing more and nothing less. God promised it if we do it, therefore if we do it, we have a right to get it. If the Protestant will admit that God has promised salvation to those who do His will, then this concedes the entire issue, for this is all that merit entails in Catholic teaching. A person might not like using the word this way, and we might agree with them in their distaste for such language - but truth is sometimes bitter (Rev. 10:9-10). If God has made this promise, then we have to accept the doctrine of merit as it is defined here. However

---

points, and far too "spiritual". Likewise, when apologists and scholars try to make merit into something that accrues to us because of the intrinsic value of Christ's works within us, I fear they are guilty of this same sort of, slightly erroneous, over-mystifying of the truth, that ultimately does more harm than good, leading people away from, rather than towards, Catholic truth. It sounds good and mystical and spiritual, but it's really just highfalutin (albeit good intentioned).

[50] Even carnal works would be meritorious if God promised recompense to them.

disfavorable we might find it, the language of merit is biblical: Salvation is a prize we win by running the race, a reward we merit by doing God's will (1 Cor. 9:24, etc.). A more in-depth treatment of the various biblical passages which speak of merit is found in the previous chapter devoted to Scripture. And for more on the ability of Catholics to simultaneously affirm merit, while distancing themselves from the use of such language, see the section entitled "Emphasis and Infallibility" at the end of this chapter.

Grace in Merit

The analogy for merit given in the previous section is incomplete and inadequate because it fails to highlight how merit is all grace. We established merit, but we didn't make it fully clear exactly how it is compatible with *sola fide*. In order to see the fully-orbed biblical doctrine, the necessity of grace from start to finish needs to be emphasized. It is impossible to exaggerate in this regard. At the start, God made a promise of salvation - this is already of astounding grace. We have all sinned against God, turned our backs on Him, rejected Him, and kicked Him out of our world. When He came to visit us in our own form, we spit on Him, tortured Him to death on a cross. Humanity deserves nothing but unending separation from His majesty and all the torment that alienation entails. There is no work we could have done to merit the possibility of redemption. Yet He promised it to us. God did not leave us with our just desserts, but mercifully condescended to us, and made this promise to us, promising to give us eternal life if we only turn from our self-destructive ways and say yes: if only we say 'yes' to life and life more abundantly. But this promise wasn't easy for God to make. He didn't just decide to grace us despite our not deserving it. He also, and most importantly, had to become one of us, and allow us to brutally torture Him to death on the cross in order to atone for our sins to make it possible. The promise made to us was paid for with the price of God's own blood.

Already the kind of merit we are talking about has been reduced to a mere shadow of anything which could allow someone to boast. But there is more to this story. God died for our sins, and made us a promise we did no works to merit (indeed, could not do any works to merit). But we are rebellious sinners and don't even want the promise. We don't want life with God. We don't want true love. We prefer sin and self-destruction. No human would ever repent, nor even desire salvation, but would only ever embrace their own alienation from God and its terrible consequences, if God did not reach down into our miserable little hearts, and by His grace, awaken us to the beauty of

His love, and inspire us to desire life with Him. When we repent and say yes, we merit what He has promised, but the analogy of promising a trillion dollars for a water bottle needs to be supplemented with the detail that no one would ever want the trillion dollars to begin with. And even if we wanted it, we don't have the ability to get the water bottle anyway. Even if a person wanted salvation, they would be utterly incapable of actually repenting and saying yes, apart from grace first coming and inspiring them to do so. God has to illuminate our hearts and minds so that we desire salvation, and then enable and empower our limbs to get up and to walk across the street to get the water bottle; and then He has to give us the money to buy it, and continue strengthening us to walk back across the street, and then move within our arms, by His grace, to enable us to extend the water bottle back out to Himself. There is no step, from desiring salvation, to repenting, to receiving the gift, which is possible apart from grace. This does not happen apart from our will assenting to and cooperating with His grace, but our will is incapable of even desiring this, let alone doing it, apart from His constant supply of grace coming before, enabling, and inspiring us to do so.

It now becomes clear the sort of merit we are talking about. It is merit, for God has made the promise, but this is all grace. "God crowns His own gifts." From start to finish: the promise, the means by which it was made possible, the impetus within us to actually want it, the ability to carry out that desire, are all from God. Our cooperation with this grace is made into merit by the God who took captivity captive and gives good gifts to men (Eph. 4:7-8). As the Council of Trent teaches, in the very same line it teaches merit, "God forbid that a Christian should either trust or glory in himself, and not in the Lord, whose bounty towards all men is so great, that He will have the things which are His own gifts be their merits." Because merit is based on grace, it gives no basis for boasting in or trusting in self, but only in the Lord who gives it. There was no good work we could do to merit the promise in the first place, the blood of Christ was the price God paid to make it, and apart from grace inspiring us to want salvation, and enabling us to say yes to it, none of our works would ever be capable of receiving it.

Merit for Protestants

If what we have been saying about the existence and nature of merit is objectionable to Protestant ears, the first recourse would be going to the previous chapter on Scripture where I have laid out some of the biblical passages which undergird this teaching. A second appeal may also be helpful, in that many of the earliest Protestants, and Protestant scholars since, have been willing to agree with us that merit of this nature exists. In the selection below from Phillip Melanchthon's Loci communes, he goes as far as saying that we can not only merit the reward of salvation due to God's grace and promise, but even that God has made Himself a debtor and put Himself under obligation to those who have faith:

> You will say: "Then we merit nothing at all? Why does Scripture so often use the word 'reward'?" It is a reward and should be, not because of any merit on our own, but because the Father has promised, and as it were, already bound Himself under obligation to us, and made Himself a debtor to them that have merited nothing of the kind... eternal life (is) a gift, not a debt, although it is a debt, because the Father has promised it, and has put His faith under obligation to us.

Salvation is a reward not because of any intrinsic merit of our own, says Melanchthon? True, and that's the Catholic teaching, too. Nothing about us or our works merit salvation on their own. They do not possess such intrinsic value. It is only because God has made the superabundant promise to us, that the reward is made possible. Remember our previous analogy. Getting the bottle of water does not intrinsically merit a trillion dollars. Yet because God made the promise, if we do it, we merit it. Once this is understood about Catholic merit, that it is all grace, nothing should prevent biblically-sensitive Protestants from being able to embrace it as orthodox. God has promised salvation as a gift of His grace to all those who repent and place their faith in Him; ipso facto, as Melanchthon said: *"Eternal life is a gift, not a debt; although it is a debt because the Father has promised it."*

Dialectic

What is this dialectic we speak of? Some history will help, for in the history of philosophy we learn of a bewildering phenomenon between the time of Parmenides and Aristotle. During those centuries the world's great intellectuals were caught up in a frustration and confusion of logic, for Parmenides had convinced them that there is only one thing in all of reality, and that there is never any change or division within it: there is no such thing as "this or that", there is only "this". There is nothing that is in any way "not," for there is only that which is. According to Parmenides, it makes no sense to predicate any difference between things, or any form of "not being" to anything that exists, for there is only one thing in all of existence, and anything that "is" cannot not be. For example, one cannot say "an apple is not a giraffe," because an apple "is," and what "is" cannot "not be". To "not be" a giraffe makes no sense for an apple, because an apple "is." If an apple "is" then it cannot not be (even if we are merely saying it "is not" a giraffe). In short, it is nonsensical to attribute "not being" in any way to "being."

These word games seem very silly and confusing. But this linguistic confusion of logic troubled philosophers until the time of Aristotle, when he finally explained how something can "be" in one sense and "not be" in another. What on the surface appears like a contradiction is perfectly reconcilable. An apple "is" in the sense that it exists, but "is not" in the sense that it's not a giraffe. Very simple, elementary stuff, we think today. But take for example this claim: My car is both white and not-white. While on the surface it seems contradictory, this is actually true, for my car is pearl white, and pearl white is not really simply white, but a variant of it. But if I had not explained the distinction, one would think I was speaking nonsense by saying my car is both white and not-white.

Now what does all this have to do with the Bible? Take a look at Prov. 26:4-5:

> Answer not a fool according to his folly, or you will be like him. Answer a fool according to his folly, or he will be wise in his own eyes.

What can this possibly mean? Do *not* answer a fool according to his folly - *Do* answer a fool according to his folly? These two statements directly contradict each other. They say the exact opposite thing. Both "do" and "do not" answer a fool according to their folly. Of course, Scripture does not contradict itself. But, as this passage shows, it's language sometimes can. This particular Proverb conveys a wise and prudent teaching about not sinking to the level of others, but instead showing them the error of their ways. But the language Scripture uses to convey this message is contradictory. "Do this - don't do this." And this isn't the only example. Our Lord teaches: *"fear not those who can kill the body, but fear him who after the body is dead can cast the soul into hell"* and then follows it up with *"fear not, for it is your Father's good pleasure to give you the kingdom."* At the same time, in the same passage: fear God - don't fear God. Likewise, Paul can say that we are justified by faith alone and not by works, and James can say, *"we are justified by works and not by faith alone"* (2:24). In one passage salvation is a wage we cannot merit (Rom. 4:4-5), in another it is the reward we can only merit by finishing the race (1 Cor. 9:24), and in another a wage we earn by working for God (Matthew 20).

In speaking of dialectic here, we are of course not speaking of a violation of the law of non-contradiction (indeed, in the long and varied history of the philosophy of dialectic, I know of no one, not even Hegel, who understood it in such terms). The meaning is a conversation between two points of view which *seem* to be in contradiction - not which actually are. The contradiction is linguistic, not substantive. It is the dialogue between two points of view that seem to contradict each other, but are merely in tension and which actually complement each other and help round each other out. Without an awareness of how the differing points of view work together, one can easily think they are just at odds with each other. How can an apple be [an apple] and not be [a giraffe] at the same time?

It is precisely a failure to appreciate the biblical dialectic that prevents so many people from understanding how the Bible can say "this is" and "this is not" at the same time; how it can say "do answer a fool according to his folly" and "do not answer a fool according to his folly" in the same proverb; how both "by faith alone, not by works or merit" and "by works and merit, not by faith alone" can be true at the same time. Some want to say, "if *sola fide* is true, then merit cannot exist" - but this betrays a deficient understanding of biblical dialectic, and of Scripture's varied ways of speaking about salvation.

Sola Fide and Merit

The dialectic of salvation is between two views: one, we are saved by faith alone and not by good works or merits; and two, that we must earn our salvation. My Catholic readers have just cringed (we must "earn" our salvation?) - and devout Protestants have all but stopped reading. Admittedly, the phrasing here, "we must earn our salvation," is pointed, and meant to invoke a reaction. But we have already parsed out what merit means, and its nature as being "all grace." If a person agrees that God has promised salvation to those who repent, then they have conceded the validity of the language just used. That is all that is meant by saying "we must earn our salvation" - that the only way to be saved is by repenting of sin. And if you repent, you merit what God has promised to those who do. The biblical dialectic says this: in one sense, salvation is by faith alone and cannot be earned; and in another sense, the only way to be saved is earning it. In the following paragraphs I will explain why each sense is true, and how the two senses work together.

When I teach salvation in parish catechesis or in Catholic schools, I begin by asking a question, "why did God create humanity?" Instead of just providing the answer, I take the opportunity to expand on the divine attributes. Specifically, God is infinitely and eternally blissful; always has been, always will be. There is nothing that could change His infinite, perfect, eternal nature. He is Triune, not alone or lonely, but in eternal companionship and perfect love with Himself, infinitely satisfied and content, from before all Creation, with no need of anything. He could create a trillion universes with trillions of trillions of creatures in each of them, all constantly offering Him sacrifices and praise, constantly offering Him endless friendship and company, and none of that would make His already infinite bliss and contentment any greater. After emphasizing this about God, I ask again: so why did God create? Was there anything He could gain from it? Of course not - He created us out of pure generosity. God is unfathomable love and happiness and goodness and beauty and truth, and He wanted to create people to enjoy Him. He wants and needs nothing from us, but simply wants to give us life and help us enjoy it (Him) forever.

To help explain this point, I speak of my own relationship with my nieces and nephews. I love these kids, but there is nothing they can do for me, nothing they can give me. Sure, I may want a new car, or a home gym, or various other things. But they can't give me any of that. They are children, not even yet teenagers. They have no money. They have no skills to make me anything of substance (though Brody, at the age of 6, could do things on a skateboard I wasn't able to do in my prime, and Cooper, at 7, already has more tackles in one game than I ever tallied up). And yet, when I go visit them, say on a birthday or some other event, I will bring them gifts. Why? What am I intending to get in return? The only reason, of course, is because I want to make them happy. I want to put a smile on their face. There is no condition they need to fulfill in order to receive the gift - nothing I require of them. The only thing they need to do is say "yes" to my offer by receiving the gift I want to give them. As long as they will receive it, it's theirs to have; as long as they want it, it's theirs. I *want* to give it to them, after all. I want them to have it.

This is what salvation is like. God doesn't want or need anything from us. He cannot benefit from us. He experiences no additional happiness if we worship Him. He is God. He is already infinitely happy and has everything He could ever want (if it even makes sense to speak this way). All He wants to do in relation to us, is to give us the gift of life and help us enjoy it (Him) forever. He wants us to live. He wants us to be happy. As our Lord Jesus tells us, *"Fear not, little children, for it is your Father's good pleasure to give you the kingdom"* (Luke 12:32). In fact, God wants our salvation infinitely more than we want it for ourselves. He wants us to have life so badly, with such an intense passion, that He was willing to become man and be brutally tortured to death in order for us to have it. Will He who died to save us, reject anyone of us who is willing to receive what He paid so high a price to give us? Once we see all of this, it becomes abundantly clear that the only condition for salvation, is to simply say "yes" and receive it. That is to say, there is no condition at all: the condition to receive is that you be willing to receive. It's free for the taking, for everyone who will take it. Christ's arms are wide open. This is the primary and fundamental truth undergirding the *sola fide* side of the dialectic of salvation: Salvation is a gift of the pure generosity and goodness of the Lord. He wants us to have it. There is nothing required except that we say yes.

Sola fide is undergirded not just by the gratuitousness of salvation, but also by the supernatural character of it. There is nothing within human power that could create, sustain, or resurrect life from the dead. It is completely outside of our power to in any way acquire a relationship with God. Salvation is "not by works" because there are no works we can do to save ourselves. We cannot achieve it or earn it through our own efforts. At every moment in our life, no matter how progressed in the spiritual life we may be, we are completely and utterly dependent upon God for our very existence, and for every good thing that exists within us. There will never be a moment in all of eternity when our continued existence isn't solely a matter of God's sustaining power. Not only does God benefit nothing from our works, but they are utterly impotent in this regard. There is no amount of fasting, praying, offering up sacrifices, charitable giving, or any other form of good works that we could do to forgive ourselves, regenerate our souls, or in any way give ourselves life. Life is a gift of God, and only He can give it. We cannot acquire it through our own efforts.

Salvation is by faith alone, and not by works, for this reason too: because all have sinned. No one has any good works by which they could be saved to begin with, because everyone's works, when balanced on the scales of justice, will be found lacking. Yet in the midst of our guilt, God came down to earth, became one of us, and allowed us to torture Him to death on the Cross to save us. If in our pride we cling to ourselves, refuse to recognize our need for Jesus - if we think we need to, or can, by our own efforts, descend into the depths of Sheol, grab our own dead carcass, resurrect ourselves, and bring about our own salvation, then we have a fundamental misunderstanding of our guilt, inability, and dependence on grace. Christ has won and done all these things for us: *"Do not say in your heart, 'who will descend/ascend', as if it depended on your effort, as if Christ has not done these things for you, and offers them by grace through faith to you"* (my interpretation of Rom. 10:5-10). The one who looks to their own works looks to the Cross, mocking Christ, "What are you doing up there? Come down from that Cross, I don't need you, I can save myself." An insistence upon our own works amounts to a self-righteous refusal and prideful denial of our own guilt and inability; and the one who comes to God pleading their own merits, will find they have none: their only option was to plead the merits of another. Only the blood of Christ can make us capable of standing before God. We must humbly accept His vicarious death on our behalf, not pleading our own righteousness, but receiving the righteousness of God as a gift of His Son, through faith alone, and not through our own works and merits.

These things come together to form the biblical and Catholic doctrine of *sola fide*, salvation by grace through faith and not my works or merit. There is nothing sinful humans can do to save themselves. But God in His infinite love, mercy, and grace, offers forgiveness, restoration, and eternal life to us all, freely, as a gift, to all who will simply say 'yes' in faith. Attempts to achieve this, to establish yourself as righteous, to save yourself, are sinful denials of grace. Only the "empty-hand" of faith, which comes before God not clinging to a deranged idea of creaturely independence from God, but fully open to grace, can receive salvation. There is no condition but a 'yes' to God. This alone can save us. Nothing else can. And this alone is eternally sufficient.

But salvation is by works and merit, and not by faith alone, because merely knowing that God is good, that He died for you and promises you eternal life, doesn't mean you actually want what He is offering. There will be people on the day of judgment day who trusted that Christ was going to bring them to Heaven, because they knew that Christ died for them, but despite knowing this and trusting this, never actually loved God more than sin. They didn't even *want* to love God more than sin. They never repented. They told themselves "Christ loves me so much and died for me, He will surely save me, therefore I can sin all I want," and thus their faith possessed no saving power. They remained enemies of the life of God. They cared more about money, carnal pleasure, reputation, pride in self, or some other created thing, than they cared about God. We say nothing about being free from sin - they didn't even *want* to be free of sin, they didn't want to live the life God is offering in salvation. No matter how much faith and trust such a person may have, they remain alienated from salvation. You could bring them into Heaven - but for them, the love of God would only burn like Hell. They cry out, "Lord Jesus! Lord Jesus!" and even do miracles in His name, but apart from repentance, they find only outer darkness.

The eternal life that is offered us in salvation is not an eternal 'existence' in abstract terms. It is eternal *life*. It is true life: life in God, in love, beauty, truth, and goodness. It is life in Heaven. Heaven is a community of perfect harmony and fellowship with God, with ourselves, and with the angels and Saint. God is not offering us an eternity of freedom to sin, but freedom from sin. Freedom from the destruction, misery, greed, and hatred of sin. In order to actually want this gift, in order to actually say 'yes' in faith and receive it, we must sincerely want to live the life God is offering. If we set our will on sin, to behave in ways destructive to ourselves and to communion with God and fellowship with others, then we have set our wills against salvation itself. We may want "heaven," but we don't want Heaven. We aren't saying yes to God. We are saying yes to sin and self in a manner that alienates us from love, from God, from others, and indeed, even from the very self we were seeking to find. The "yes" of faith finds self by losing self in God. For us sinners this "yes" of faith, though simple, isn't easy. We are inclined towards sin, and to say "yes" to life without sin is only possible by grace. This turning from sin and saying yes to God is something we must "do" by grace. We must repent. We must say no to the carnal pleasures of sin that entice us to turn away from God; and we must persevere in the sometimes painful and difficult way of righteousness, treasuring God above everything the world can offer.

For this reason, the "yes" of *sola fide* involves a necessary life of difficult "doings", the doings of avoiding and resisting temptation, and of strengthening our resolve in the will of God. And God has promised that if we do this, He will give us eternal life. Not because He needs or wants anything from us, but because for us to say "yes" to what God is offering, involves all these things. The desire for salvation involves distaste for sin that destroys life and a 'yes' to the love and fellowship that defines it. For those who embrace an orientation of the heart that treasures life with God above the love of self, there is an assurance and guarantee of salvation. This is promised. As long as a person wants it, it is theirs. Those who set their hearts on our Lord Jesus thereby merit the promise - the promise being nothing other than the majestic Lord Himself.

This is the dialectic of *sola fide* and merit: All that salvation requires is 'yes;' this alone can receive it, and this alone is eternally sufficient. There is nothing else we could do to earn or achieve it, and to trust in our own works, as if we deserve it, or could attain it on our own, is to contradict the grace offered us in Jesus. At the same time, salvation requires that we repent and do all those things necessary to remain repentant until we die. And if we do that, we merit what God has promised to those who do - not, importantly, because anything more than "yes" is required, but because all of that "doing" is caught up in it.

Only those who persevere till the end will be saved - but God promises salvation to those who do. We can rest assured that those who finish the race will merit the promise; for God is not unjust, nor will He forget our work. Even if we have only labored for but a single moment upon our deathbed, we will merit the same wage as those who have toiled in the noonday sun. So, we have this dialectic: salvation is a gift of God that we cannot acquire or achieve for ourselves, but can only receive through faith alone. Insisting upon our own works is a self-righteous denial of grace which rejects the Cross - only the empty-hand which does not cling to its own works and merits can receive the gift, and it is guaranteed to receive it. This faith, this yes to God, and this alone, saves us, and is eternally sufficient for salvation. God requires nothing more, for God wants us to have it. But merely believing these things are true is not enough. One must actually want to live in Heaven. One must actually want to love God and be free from sin. Though simple, this is not easy for us sinners. We have to resist temptations and persevere in the will of God to be saved. If we do that, we will merit what God has promised to those who do. *Sola fide* and merit, then, form this dialectic. Those who seek their life will lose it, but those who lose their life will find it. We cannot look to our own works and merits for salvation, but by denying ourselves and looking to Christ, who offers it to us freely, we thereby do the work necessary to merit and receive it.

The Dialectic in Augustine

The primary reason I am displaying this dialectic of *sola fide* and merit is because it is true, and I want people to know the truth. A secondary reason is because I have experienced the fruits of *sola fide* preached rightly, and I wish for my Catholic brothers and sisters to experience that same joy and sanctity, which too often, whether for anti-Protestantism, or for ignorance, they are deprived of. A third reason, of equal importance, is because I have experienced the graces of the Sacraments and of being Catholic, and I know that one reason why my Protestant friends don't come forward to experience these gifts of the Catholic Church, is because of their misgivings with regards to Catholic soteriology, and the perceived Catholic rejection of *sola fide* and the Catholic teaching on works and merit. I hope to persuade them of the orthodoxy of Catholic teaching on these points. Now for this trinity of purpose the witness of Augustine is exceedingly valuable. He is renowned even among secularists for his brilliance, and his agreement brings credibility. As a Catholic his Old Perspective reading, as well as his emphasis on salvation apart from good works and merits, by grace and faith alone, should bring my fellow Catholics closer to these views. As beloved by Protestants, his affirmation of merit and the dialectic of salvation will hopefully help my Protestant family come deeper into the fullness of Catholic truth.

The fact Augustine can be marshaled as an example here may surprise some. For example, Michael Horton begins a discussion of the Saint by pointing out that, although the Latin translator of Origen's work, Rufinus, had sided with Pelagius over against Augustine, that nevertheless, Origen's affirmation of merit was an understandable "overreaction" to his gnostic opponents. This leads readers to believe that Augustine stood in stark contrast with Origen's affirmation of merit, something Horton implies elsewhere in the same series:

> By the third century the word 'merit' was being used interchangeably with 'reward.' Tertullian writes, "Again, we affirm that a judgment has been ordained by God according to the merits of every man." "A good deed has God for its debtor," he writes elsewhere…this statement contrasts sharply with Augustine's statement, "The Lord made himself a debtor not be receiving something, but by promising something. One does not say to him, 'Pay for what you received,' But 'Pay what you promised.'"[51]

And while there are hundreds of passages in Augustine, like the one above, that speak negatively of merit, setting justification and grace in opposition with it, there are also plenty of instances in which Augustine affirms merit - even the possibility of meriting eternal life itself. For example, from his *Sermon 11*,

---

[51] Michael Horton, *Justification* (Grand Rapids: Zondervan, 2018). The bit about Origen is in the first volume, p. 84; the extended citation is from the second, p. 344. It should be noted that the text cited from Tertullian, On Repentance, actually affirms the grace-based, promise-enabled nature of merit: "And so He gathered together a people for Himself, and fostered them with many liberal distributions of His bounty…By and by, promising freely the grace which in the last times He was intending to pour as a flood of light on the universal world through His Spirit, He bade the baptism of repentance lead the way…through grace, to (inherit) the promise surely made to Abraham….bringing salvation according to God's promise…This is the (final) cause of repentance, this her work, in taking in hand the business of divine mercy…For God, never giving His sanction to the reprobation of good deeds, inasmuch as they are His own (of which, being the author, He must necessarily be the defender too), is in like manner the acceptor of them, and if the acceptor, likewise the rewarder. Let, then, the ingratitude of men see to it, if it attaches repentance even to good works; let their gratitude see to it too, if the desire of earning it be the incentive to well-doing: earthly and mortal are they each. For how small is your gain if you do good to a grateful man! Or your loss if to an ungrateful! A good deed has God as its debtor, just as an evil has too; for a judge is rewarder of every cause."

When the devout servants of God are sometimes in need, while they are giving all their time to God unceasingly, those who have the wealth of this world are generous with alms to them. As they share with them their earthly substance, so with them they will merit a share in eternal life.

And here in *Sermon 15*, it is implied that Abraham's salvation was contingent on merit:

The poor man is raised up to the bosom of a rich man. If his merit lay precisely in his poverty, then Abraham would not have preceded him into eternal rest, to welcome him when he followed. But because the same thing was found in the poor man Lazarus as in the rich man Abraham, namely humility, neither riches were a hindrance to the one nor poverty to the other, but the merit of both was their piety.

In Augustine's understanding we are saved apart from merits because merits cannot precede grace. But once grace has been established, merit then becomes possible. In *Sermon 169*:

Grace came before your deserving, or merit; it isn't grace coming from merit, but merit from grace. Because if grace comes from merit, it means you have bought it, not received it free, gratis, for nothing. For nothing, it says, you will save them (Ps. 56:7). What's the meaning of For nothing you will save them? You can find no reason in them to save them, and yet you save them. You give for nothing, you save for nothing. You precede all merits, so that my merits follow your gifts.

And in his *On Faith and Works* he says that doing the "works of the law" is meritorious after justification:

When St. Paul says, therefore, that man is justified by faith and not by the observance of the law [Rom. 3:28]. He does not mean that good works are not necessary or that it is enough to receive and to profess the faith and no more. What he means rather and what he wants us to understand is that man can be justified by faith, even though he has not previously performed any works of the law. For the works of the law are meritorious not before but after justification.

Michael Horton quoted Augustine's, *'The Lord made himself a debtor not by receiving something, but by promising something. One does not say to him, 'Pay for what you received,'*

But *Pay what you promised,"* and Horton used this quote to set distance between the Saint and the concept of merit, but the fuller context of the same quote does the exact opposite. From *Sermon 158,*

> As regards those, you see, which we already have, we must praise God our generous benefactor; as regards those we don't yet have, we must hold him as our debtor. He became our debtor, you see, not by receiving anything from us, but by promising us what he pleased. It is not, after all, the same thing to say to someone, "You owe it to me, because I have given you something," as to say, "You owe it to me, because you promised it to me." When you say, "You owe it to me, because I have given you something," the benefit has come from you, but as a loan, not a gift. When, however, you say, "You owe it to me, because you promised it to me," you yourself have given nothing, and yet you are demanding something. And the goodness of the one who made you the promise will give it to you, or else trust would turn into spite. To cheat on a promise, after all, is spiteful. Now can we say to God, "Pay me back, because I have given you something?" What have we given to God, seeing that everything we are, and everything good that we have, we have from him? So we have given him precisely nothing. There is no way we can use that tone of voice in making demands on God as our debtor, especially as the apostle tells us, For who has known the mind of the Lord? Or who has been his adviser? Or who ever first gave to him, and will be repaid? (Rom 11:34-35). So the only way we can make demands on our Lord, is by saying, "Give us what you have promised, because we have done what you told us to; and it's you that have done even this, because you helped us when we found it difficult."

This is the exact sort of merit the Catholic Church affirms: a merit based on the promise of God. But the Church would rarely ever state the concept as strongly as Augustine has here, that "God is our debtor." And while many of my Catholic readers would disfavor associating the word "earn" with the concept of merit, Augustine (or at least his translator) does not seem to mind. See the end of this excerpt from Sermon 348a,

> Much more, it says, being justified now. By what means? By his blood, not by our own powers, not by our own merits, but by his blood, shall we be saved from the wrath through him,

not through ourselves, but through him. He has tied us up to the cross; assuredly, if we want to live, let us cling to that death. If you cling to yourself, you are clinging to death; life, after all, is not be found in one who is dead. Why, being dead, do you rely on yourself? You were able to die of your own accord, you cannot come back to life of your own accord. We were able to sin by ourselves, and we are still able to, nor shall we ever not be able to. Let our hope be in nothing but in God. Let us send up our sighs to him, let us rely on him; as for ourselves, let us strive with our wills to earn merit by our prayers.

In the same context that Augustine says we are not justified by our merits and works, he exhorts us to earn merit for ourselves. This is the dialectic we have been laboring to show. Both 'not by merit' and 'by merit' at the same time, and here by Augustine in the very same passage. Elsewhere, in the *Enchiridion*, he does the same thing, but more dramatically. In chapter 99 of the work, he says that the only difference between the saved and the damned is grace alone, and not any merits or demerits on their part: *"neither can he that is pardoned glory in any merit of his own, nor he that is condemned complain of anything but his own demerit. For it is grace alone that separates the redeemed from the lost";* and yet in chapter 110 of the same work, he says that your salvation is determined by the merits you "earn" during your earthly life:

These services are of advantage only to those who during their lives have earned such merit, that services of this kind can help them. For there is a manner of life which is neither so good as not to require these services after death, nor so bad that such services are of no avail after death; there is, on the other hand, a kind of life so good as not to require them; and again, one so bad that when life is over they render no help. Therefore, it is in this life that all the merit or demerit is acquired, which can either relieve or aggravate a man's sufferings after this life. No one, then, need hope that after he is dead he shall obtain merit with God which he has neglected to secure here.

In the same work Augustine first says salvation is by grace alone and not by merits or demerits, and then follows it up a few chapters later by saying that salvation is determined by whether you have lived good enough to earn merit or bad enough to have acquired demerit. Salvation in one case is by grace alone and apart from anything within the redeemed or the lost which would differentiate them, such as merits or demerits. Salvation in the other case is determined by whether you behaved well and earned merit or behaved badly and acquired demerit.

In one place you can find Augustine using the language of *sola fide*, as seen here in Sermon 2:

> Abraham believed God and it was reckoned to him as justice, and he was called God's friend. That he believed God deep in his heart is a matter of faith alone. But that he took his son to sacrifice him…(was) a great work. And God praised the work when he said, "Because you have listened to my voice." So why does the apostle Paul say, We reckon that a man is justified by faith without the works of the law?… Consider carefully just how, brothers. Somebody believes, receives the sacraments of faith in bed, and is dead. He had no time to do works. What are we to say? That he was not justified? Of course we say he was justified, by believing in him who justifies the wicked (Rom 4:5). So this person is justified without having done any work.

But affirmations of *sola fide* such as these do not stop him from elsewhere also teaching that faith alone is insufficient. From Sermon 16a,

> And there you have before you Christ as your end. You have no need to go on looking anymore. The moment you have believed, you have already recognized it. But it isn't just a matter of faith, but of faith and works. Each is necessary. For the demons also believe—you heard the apostle — and tremble (Jas 2:19); but their believing doesn't do them any good. Faith alone is not enough, unless works too are joined to it: "Faith working through love" (Gal 5:6), says the apostle.

And in *On Faith and Works*, he writes as well,

> I do not see why the Lord said, "if you will enter life, keep the commandments" if one can obtain eternal life by faith alone…(but) in order that no one might think that a faith without works is sufficient for eternal life.[52]

---

[52] Augustine, *On Faith and Works* (New York: Newman Press, 1988), 32.

And yet, in *Spirit and Letter,* writes that,

> Man is not justified by the precepts of a holy life, but by faith
> in Jesus Christ — in a word, not by the law of works, but by
> the law of faith; not by the letter, but by the spirit; not by the
> merits of deeds, but by free grace.

These various statements can appear to contradict each other. Salvation is by
faith alone, and not by works. But faith alone is not enough... indeed no one
can obtain eternal life by faith alone. Except that, man is not justified by a holy
life, but by faith - not by the merit of deeds, but by free grace. While such
statements seem contradictory, they in fact work together to complete the well-
rounded, biblical picture of salvation. In one sense, *sola fide*, in another, we must
work. This is the dialectic of salvation, *sola fide* and merit, that the Catholic
Church and the Sacred Scriptures both witness. Salvation is both "by faith alone
apart from good works," and also "by works and not by faith alone". We cannot
earn salvation, but in God's grace we can. We must. While my synthesis of this
dialectic is perhaps new, Augustine (and the host of Catholic Saints throughout
history, and the biblical data itself) show that my affirmation of the interplay is
not.

Initial Justification Only?

Of those Catholic apologists who are happy to affirm a certain form
of *sola fide*, it is almost always the case that they qualify it so as to confine it to
"initial justification" only. That is, they affirm that *sola fide* is true, but only with
regard to how a person is initially brought into relationship with God, but not,
they say, when it comes to maintaining justification and to final judgment.
These people are aware that a person's conversion and entrance into a state of
forgiveness is due to the grace of God and not their own merit or works, but
because they see in Scripture, and in the teaching of the Church, the possibility
of merit, and the ability to increase righteousness through good works, they
think they must therefore deny the relevance of *sola fide* for progressive and
final justification. "Faith alone might get you in, but it's not sufficient to keep
you in" - so they basically say.

Now we must affirm along with such people that there is a sense in
which faith is not the only instrument through which righteousness and
salvation can be received. When a Christian does by the grace of God those
things which God commands, they by those works grow in holiness
(righteousness) and, ultimately, can merit salvation. However, this does not

mean that *sola fide*, and all it stands for, ceases to have relevance for the Christian once they are justified. It is not as if the 'empty-hand of faith' which must come to God in conversion, can suddenly clinch down upon its own works and merits, and trust in these rather than God, after a person has been justified. The Council of Trent forbade, in the same passage that it affirmed the existence of merit, that a Christian should ever trust in such things: "God forbid that a Christian should either trust or glory in himself, and not in the Lord." Let us repeat ourselves: in the same passage that the Council of Trent taught the possibility of merit, it forbids Christians from trusting in it. Clearly, then, at least this aspect of *sola fide* - the pastoral aspect which warns the believer, "do not say in your heart, 'God saved me because of my own works and merit'" - at least this aspect of *sola fide*, the "empty-hand of faith", remains eternally relevant for the Christian, no matter how justified they may be.

That good works play a role after justification does not mean they can be trusted in. The Catechism quotes Therese of Lisieux on this point. The most lovely of religious sisters, steeped in grace, speaks about her final judgment in the following manner: "*In the evening of life I shall appear before you with empty hands, for I am not asking you, Lord, to count my works.*" The Catechism cites this in its section on merit as an example of the disposition Christians should have with regards their worthiness before God. Even though you may be advanced a trillion lightyears into the highest stages of mystical poverty, charity, and asceticism, absolutely steeped in the Sacraments and filled with the most pure of grace, objectively overflowing with superabundant merits, you are nevertheless exhorted to appear before God with empty-hands, not pleading your own works or righteousness, but depending on His mercy and grace alone. When Catholic apologists want to confine the application of *sola fide* to initial justification, they run the risk of misleading people about this most important spiritual truth. We must always be trusting in God alone, and never in our own works or merits.

In addition to heeding the pastoral aspect of *sola fide*, it is also the case that the theological grounding requires more careful attention here. Let us recall how the Council of Trent defined justification as relating to the whole enterprise of righteousness before God. But there is good reason to believe that Paul's simply forensic usage of the word in the relevant biblical texts denotes something more like a "basic" justification, a linear yes-or-no, foundational sort of reality about the Christian's right legal standing (acquittal) and relationship with God.[53] Now let's be clear: we are not saying Trent was

---

[53] For examples Catholic scholars who have affirmed that Paul's definition of

wrong. But there is nothing in Catholic teaching that prevents us from developing a supplemental theology of justification based on this other Pauline definition of the word, as long as this understanding stays consistent with what Trent says. Again, we are arguing that while the Council of Trent defined justification in its own particular way, and that it was not in error, that nevertheless Paul likewise had his own unique and specific definition. There is not substantial disagreement between the two in terms of theology, but they are (or seem to be) using the words differently. With this in mind, if we define justification as Paul did, as a basic foundational reality, a yes-or-no about our legal acquittal and standing with God, and recognize that "increases in justification" and the ability to merit salvation, are both *additive* in nature, then we can speak of a *sola fide* that is true beyond initial justification, even for final judgment, not just pastorally with regard to the required humble disposition of heart that trusts in Christ alone, but also in regard to the theoretical aspects of instrumentality: we can speak of a justification by 'faith alone' from start to finish in the Christian life.

There are a couple of reasons why this is possible. First, it is not as if Catholic dogma teaches that the faith which initially justifies (repentance/fide, caritata, formata) ever loses its salvific power. It is not as if God says, "repentance was enough to get you into right standing, but now that you have been justified for ten years, repentance no longer suffices." No, the faith that initially justifies (repentance) is more than sufficient for progressive and final justification as well. Repentance and love for God always suffice, even after ten thousand years. When a Catholic says something like "faith alone suffices to get you in, but not to keep you in" they thus seem to be equivocating the definition of faith. They seem to think that if they were to admit faith is sufficient for staying justified, this would imply continual repentance from sin unnecessary. But if that was the faith in question, they should have denied that faith was sufficient even for initial justification - since a faith that lacks repentance neither "gets one in" nor keeps one in. But repentance is always sufficient, both for getting in, and keeping one in a right relationship with God. Therefore, what suffices for initial justification - repentance - always suffices

---

justification denoted a non-progressive legal acquittal that differed from Trent's linguistics without denying the theology thereof, see the dissertation of James B. Prothro, "Both Judge and Justifier: Biblical Legal Language and the Act of Justifying in Paul," as well as the many books and articles written on this subject by Fr. Joseph Fitzmyer.

for justification at every stage of the Christian life. This is perhaps why when Pope Bendict XVI affirmed 'faith alone' he did not qualify it by reference to initial justification:

> Being just simply means being with Christ and in Christ. And this suffices. Further observances are no longer necessary. For this reason Luther's phrase: "faith alone" is true, if it is not opposed to faith in charity, in love.[54]

Another reason why we are able to speak of a *sola fide* with regard to continued and final justification is because, as we said in the paragraph before last, the possibility of merit and "increases in righteousness" are both additive in nature. It is not as if the good works we do in grace can merit for us our standing in grace. We are already in grace. Thus, both merit and increases in justice are additive to the foundational, yes-or-no, basic justification we have before God. Therefore, as long as we understand faith in terms of repentance, then this basic form of Pauline justification is affected by faith, and by faith alone, from start to finish. *Sola fide* is true from start to finish: nothing more than faith can ever cause our basic standing with God, and nothing more is ever required. *Sola fide* is not just for initial justification, but is eternally relevant and sufficient. This is made even more clear when we remember that Paul's doctrine of justification was preached to people who were already justified, who were tempted to think they needed to add Torah-observance to their faith to remain justified. His doctrine of justification was therefore not being preached into a situation where initial justification was the question, but to people whose continued and final justification was being called into question. And since his "not by works" doctrine denoted not only good works, but also (even primarily) works of the Jewish law, it should be obvious that Paul was not articulating a doctrine only relevant for initial justification. The idea things like circumcision, sabbath, etc., were relevant for continued justification or final judgment was anathema in his eyes (Gal. 1:9). Paul clearly intended his teaching on justification to be relevant for the entire Christian life, not just its beginnings.

A Capitulation?

Some who hear this talk of a Catholic *"sola fide"* will protest that this is a capitulation on the part of Catholics. They will claim that the Council of Trent

---

[54] https://www.vatican.va/content/benedict-xvi/en/audiences/2008/documents/hf_ben-xvi_aud_20081119.html

rejected *sola fide* and that Catholic theologians have not so much developed or refined their position on this point as they have just changed or innovated a new stance. And it is certainly the case that our tone is strikingly different from that of the Council of Trent. But tone and substance are different things, and we have shown in the previous chapter that the chorus of Doctors of the Church and Catholic Saints have always understood the Pauline doctrine of justification by faith apart from good works in terms of a certain *sola fide*. The substance of what we mean by *sola fide* in this book has been amply explained: we are not denying that good works can, in a sense, increase justification; nor are we denying that good works can, in a sense, merit eternal life; nor are we denying that the formal cause of justification is infused righteousness (see the last chapter on Imputation); nor are we trying to affirm a form of *sola fide* which asserts that confidence in one's salvation guarantees one's salvation, as Lutherans and many evangelicals claim it does.

Everything we have been affirming about *sola fide* is, in its substance, consistent with the Council of Trent, consistent with the witness of the fathers, and has been affirmed by the highest levels of Church authority (Doctors, Saints, Popes, Catechisms, Theologians, etc.). It is impossible for a person in good faith and decent education to claim that because our language and tone have changed, this means our substance has as well. Furthermore, even if there were refinements, alterations, developments in substance, this would not be contrary to the infallibility of the Church and the Catholic faith, just so long as those changes and corrections did not contradict prior dogmas or imply there were technical errors in them. The infallibility of the Church does not guarantee that the Church will always be as helpful, as wise, as prudent, or as accurate as we wish it to be. Infallibility is a negative charism that prevents dogmas from being wrong: it does not positively inspire them to be as true or as helpful as they possibly could be. This should be obvious given the infinite nature of God and the fact that no pronouncement of the Church, even if it was positively inspired, would ever tell us everything we can and would want to know. Of course, the dogmas of the Church are open to further development, can be supplemented by extra information and nuance, etc.

But even if we think the proper emphasis in our spirituality and teaching should be more on the *sola fide* side of the dialectic than on merit and works (as we will agree with in the following section), nevertheless, it must be said, the Scriptural account decidedly weighs in favor of the latter (as we noted in the chapter on Scripture). As clear and emphatic as Paul might be about justification by faith apart from works, his testimonies on that subject make up a relatively small portion of the biblical account. If we were to count up and compare the passages which speak of salvation as being determined by what we do, and compare the number with the passages that set up an antithesis between doing and believing, the scale would fall like a rock in favor of the passages which depict our "doing" as the determinative factor of our salvation. We might not like the language of the Council of Trent, but the only time Scripture uses the language of "faith alone" it agrees: "man is justified by works and not by faith alone" (James 2). To point this out is not to recant the entire thrust of this entire book (*sola fide* is true in dialectic with merit), but to show that a biblically sensitive person should not have real difficulty swallowing the language of Trent on this point, given it is the language of Scripture. At the same time, we have labored to show over and over again, that the substance of the *sola fide* doctrine can be, and is, and always has been, consistent with Catholic dogma, just so long as *sola fide* is understood in the biblical manner. There is no novelty in this affirmation, but only a clarification now that the Church has moved past the era of hostility and confrontation with Protestantism, and is open to building bridges where they can be found. The wood for this bridge, the Catholic and biblical *sola fide*, has been in the barque of Peter throughout the ages.

In fact, while the Council of Trent took a hostile approach in its response to the Reformation, and most Catholics since then have felt an obligation to uphold the anti-Protestant approach of the Council, there not only were plenty of Catholics who before that point had understood Paul's *sola fide* in a manner similar to Luther, but there existed even in Luther's day a significant contingent of Catholics who were deeply sympathetic to his arguments, and who had nearly identical experiences involving struggles of conscience and despair over their salvation that led them to an eventual experience of the gratuitousness of salvation and assurance by faith apart from works and merits. A notable Catholic among this group was the Cardinal Gasparo Contarini. In 1511, before Luther's reformation would begin six years later, Contarini, despairing of his salvation, spoke with a Priest on Holy Saturday before Easter, who encouraged him about God's mercy and likewise prompted him to reflect on the futility of his good works. He described the turn of thinking that occurred after that conversation:

> After I left him I began to think over for myself what that salvation is, and what our condition is. And I understood only that if I did all the penances possible, and even many more,

they would not be enough at one great stroke, I shall not say
to merit that salvation, but to atone for my past sins.[55]

In light of this, Contarini eventually realized that Christ's atoning death on the
Cross was sufficient for sinners, and was filled with happiness and felt his spirit
transformed as he turned towards the outstretched arms of Christ which sought
to embrace Him, and allowed the Savior's blood to cancel the debt he himself
was incapable of satisfying:

> As regards the satisfaction for the sins committed, and into
> which human weakness falls, His passion is sufficient and
> more than sufficient. Through this thought I was changed
> from great fear and suffering to happiness. I began with my
> whole spirit to turn to this greatest good which I saw, for the
> love of me, on the cross, with his arms open, and his breast
> opened right up to his heart. Thus I, the wretch who had not
> had enough courage for the atonement of my inequities to
> leave the world and do penance, turned to him; and since I
> asked him to let me share in the satisfaction which he, without
> any sins of his own, had made for us, he was quick to accept
> me and to cause his Father to cancel the debt I had
> contracted, which I by myself was incapable of satisfying.[56]

This experience gave Contarini a profound sense of security regarding
his relationship with God and his salvation. And it was through the counsel of
a Catholic priest that young Contarini came to this awakening. Remember:
Luther did not decide to search for answers in Paul on his own. Rather, it was
Catholic Fr. Johanne Staupitz, Luther's superior in the Augustinian order, who
directed the Reformer to Paul. Throughout his life, Luther would always look
back on Fr. Staupitz and fondly refer to him as his "father in the gospel."
Although Staupitz had repeatedly admonished the young friar about God's
mercy and rebuked his scruples of conscience, Luther did not pick up what Fr.
Staupitz had been laying down. But this is worth emphasizing: just like in
Contarini's experience, the sufficiency of the Cross of Christ and the futility of
human works was something Luther did not come to on his own, but was
something he was directed towards by Catholics. Of course, some Catholics
had placed an undue emphasis on works and merit, but the evangelical
emphasis on assurance through the Cross was not absent from the Church.

---

[55] Dermot Fenlon, *Heresy and Obedience in Tridentine Italy* (Cambridge: Cambridge
University Press, 1972), 8.
[56] Ibid.

There were devout Catholics, in the highest offices of the Church, who recognized the truth in Luther's arguments about faith and works, and did not think being Catholic contradicted those truths. Cardinal Sadolet wrote to Geneva during the Reformation, arguing for the Protestant community there to come back to the Church, agreeing with them and affirming with them, that "we obtain…salvation by faith alone in God and in Jesus Christ." And even in the face of Tridentine hostility to the evangelical emphasis, men like Cardinal Pole (Contarini's spiritual companion), who so cherished the evangelical truth of the Gospel, nevertheless remained faithful to the Church, and saw nothing irreconcilable about doing so. Interestingly, Cardinal Pole thought, like Luther did, that indeed, some of his contemporary Catholics had, in their attempt to be justified by good works, committed the same error Jewish people did in Paul's day: "*even as now, there were Jews (should we wish to look around us; one may test the thing for oneself) who placed all hope of their salvation in observing the law*"[57] A Catholic expressed that sentiment then, seeing nothing un-Catholic about expressing it, and Cardinal Pole was a Catholic of such authority that he was a single vote shy of becoming Pope himself. Though he was allowed to vote for himself, he refused, and one wonders how different history might have been, and how much sooner the Church might have sought reconciliation with Protestants, had he done so.

Emphasis and Infallibility

A person who acknowledges that Scripture does at times speak of salvation in terms of a reward we merit by doing the will of God, and as being determined not just by what we believe but, in a sense by what we do, may nevertheless insist that this way of speaking about salvation is less than desirable, and because it can lead to dangerous misunderstandings, to pride, etc., that it should be avoided. Such a person's position would be more than agreeable, and there are many Catholic authorities, even since the time of Luther, who have held this position themselves. Catholics are of course free to argue that merit has been over-emphasized in the common teaching of the Church, and that pride of place should be given to justification by faith. Indeed, nothing about Catholicism implies the common preaching of the Church (lower case 't' tradition) will always be superior to the common preaching found in non-Catholic denominations. It is only a heretical breed of hyper conservatism that denies the Egyptian-origin of the Proverbs, that denies that we can learn about God from our Protestant brothers and sisters. But this is

---

[57] Ibid, 39-40.

stretching it, as we aren't here discussing polytheists who worship kittens shaped into sky-scraping monuments, but Trinitarian believers endowed with baptismal grace and the treasures of divine revelation. And the Church does not deny, but affirms, along with Scripture, that we can even learn from the fallible wisdom of the Egyptians.[58] How much more, then, can we learn from our Protestant brothers and sisters. Catholic philosopher and theologian Peter Kreeft insists that this is not just something we can do, but something that we must:

> If the teachings of the Church are true, then why doesn't God convince Protestants of those truths? I think the reason is spiritual and personal more than theological. Why should God let Protestants become Catholics when many Protestants, perhaps most, already know Christ more intimately and personally than many Catholics, perhaps most? How can God lead Protestants home to the fullness of faith in the Catholic Church until the Catholic Church becomes that fullness that they knew as Protestants, plus more? When Catholics know Christ better than Protestants do–when Catholics are better Protestants than Protestants–then Protestants will become Catholics in order to become better Protestants. When Catholics are evangelized, Protestants will be sacramentalized, but not before, evangelizing comes first.

Too often the sort of sentiment expressed by Kreeft is rejected by Catholic traditionalists as if it was a modernist concession that Protestantism is acceptable and true. They think that if Catholics agree that Protestants get some things right, and that Catholics can learn from them - that if Catholic doctrine hasn't always been preached as well as it could have been, and that Protestants have in some ways done better, that this implies that the Catholic Church isn't the infallible, one-true-Church it has always claimed to be. But this position is woefully ignorant of the entire sweep of revelation. Infallibility has never meant

---

[58] See the following from St. John Paul II, in *Fides et Ratio*, on the Book of Proverbs: "Sacred Scripture indicates with remarkably clear cues how deeply related are the knowledge conferred by faith and the knowledge conferred by reason; and it is in the Wisdom literature that this relationship is addressed most explicitly. What is striking about these biblical texts, if they are read without prejudice, is that they embody not only the faith of Israel, but also the treasury of cultures and civilizations which have long vanished. As if by special design, the voices of Egypt and Mesopotamia sound again and certain features common to the cultures of the ancient Near East come to life in these pages which are so singularly rich in deep intuition."

that dogmas are as helpful, or as prudent, or as well-stated as they could be. To be technically precise, it does not even mean they are "true" so much as it just means they aren't wrong (see the etymology: in-fallible). Catholic scholars and Saints have forever realized that dogmas can be stated in such ways that they need correction and reformation: not that they can be technically wrong, but that they can at times benefit from being parsed out and phrased in better ways; that more nuance was needed, that a different emphasis was necessary to avoid misleading people about the truth. Augustine describes how this process of correction takes place in the Church, even with regards dogmas issues by plenary/ecumenical councils: "*even of the plenary Councils, the earlier are often corrected by those which follow them, when, by some actual experiment, things are brought to light which were before concealed, and that is known which previously lay hid*" (From "On Baptism" 2.3.4). Though the existence of merit is affirmed by biblical teaching and by Church dogma, nothing about Catholicism means that merit must be emphasized, or even taught except in the confines of precise academic theology. Cardinal Avery Dulles wrote about this:

> It is regrettable that some Catholic authors, in their polemical enthusiasm, failed to guard against the dangers of merit language. Many superfluous controversies could have been avoided if a better expression had been found to convey the biblical message that promises us eternal life and entrance into the kingdom of God if we live according to the commands of God and Christ. When we do talk of merit, we would do well, Fransen reminds us, to recall that it exists only within God's covenant and on the basis of his free covenant promises. Its ground is not the works done, taken in the abstract, but rather the personal dignity of those in whom the triune God graciously takes up his dwelling. Whatever merit our deeds may have depends upon their being preceded, accompanied and followed by God's free grace. Thus it is correct to say, as did Trent, paraphrasing Augustine, that in rewarding our merits God crowns his own gifts.[59]

That quote is from Cardinal in the Catholic Church, one of the most influential and esteemed theologians of the last century, and he says that it is "regrettable" that Catholic authors "failed to guard against the dangers of merit language",

---

[59] Avery Dulles, "Justification in Contemporary Catholic Theology," in *Justification by Faith: Lutherans and Catholics in Dialogue VII* (Augsburg: Minneapolis, 1985), 274.

and that "many superfluous controversies could have been avoided if a better expression had been found."

The point of this section here is to highlight the compatibility of divine revelation with the need for theological correction, which is to say, to illustrate how infallible teachings can stand in need of modified emphasis. If our Protestant friends are willing to admit that the Scriptures speak of salvation as a reward we merit for doing the will of God, then we are already happy to agree that the emphasis should nevertheless be placed on *sola fide*. In fact, we agree with Cardinal Dulles and Peter Kreeft that the common preaching among Catholics has been deficient and regrettable, and that we can learn from our Protestant brothers and sisters how to better emphasize *sola fide* and the gratuitousness of salvation apart from works. There is much in the way of sanctity to be gained by such reformation.

Why Merit?

The use of merit-language may be regrettable, but when you read the Saints who used the language, and pay attention to the way they used it, the reason why they used it becomes apparent. They were not, of course, asserting some sort of self-entitled deservedness, or allowing for pride and self-righteousness, or boasting, or anything of that sort. While there is something of an "earned" quality about merit, the primary thing behind merit-language almost always seems to be the non-arbitrariness of God's judgment. Whereas the orthodox doctrine of *sola fide* is aimed at inculcating the empty-hand of faith, the doctrine of merit is utilized to explain why one person is saved and not another. Is there any difference between the two that merits the difference in fate? Or is God arbitrary and unjustified for saving one and not the other? Nay, judgment is indeed justified. There is an intrinsic ethical quality within the redeemed that forms the basis of the difference between them and the condemned. Unrepentant sinners get what they deserve, but those who repent and seek to live righteously merit eternal life. This is what merit language is getting at: God's judgment is not morally arbitrary. God is not partial, nor is He a respecter of persons. There is a good reason, a moral reason, why some are saved and some condemned. Merit upholds the righteousness of God's decision.

There is a sense in which only good people are saved. Repentance from sin and a heart submitted to God is necessary for salvation. Heaven is the place of the good. But there is another sense in which good people go to hell, and sinners are saved: for apart from grace all the good works you can muster can never save you, and the worst sinner in history, the moment they repent, is thereby saved to the uttermost. Furthermore, the good are only good insofar as they admit their guilt, good only insofar as they admit they are bad. But this dialectic does not vitiate the ethical component of merit and salvation, rather, it is predicated on that ethical component being present. The extent to which that ethical component should be emphasized is a question we can debate, but the existence of it is not.

Born Again Works

I have thus far written about salvation primarily in terms of the question, "what must I do to be saved?" The emphasis has been on those actions one needs to take to be saved, whether believing, or "doing," or some combination of the two. But to many, especially to my evangelical brothers and sisters, this approach may seem misguided from the start, as if I have missed the Gospel completely: for *"you must be born again."* Whether doing or believing, or whatever else is related to salvation, all come about within us only after, and because, we have been supernaturally regenerated by the Spirit of God. People who have experienced this Spirit-wrought transformation of heart and mind, and been led by grace and love for God to live a new life, can for this reason find talk about "works" misguided: the Christian believes and does good works because they have been changed and made a new person - not in order to be saved, but because they already have been. It is the supernatural transformation wrought in us by the Spirit that brings about faith, works, and everything else. And we must admit there is plenty of truth in all of this. Ideally, that is the way the Christian life is supposed to happen.

But that is "ideally." We are supposed to receive the Holy Spirit and be led by His grace to a new life in the love of Christ out of the free desires of our regenerated heart. But the reality is that we are sinners, and the work of regeneration does not eradicate all our inclinations to sin, nor does it remove our potential to sin. We have to cooperate with the Spirit, and this cooperation is not guaranteed. We have the potential to resist, to sin, to turn our backs on God, and to sever ourselves from the faith. Good works are not automatic. But this can be easily missed by people who have had a powerful conversion in the Spirit and have not fallen into sin since, and/or by those who were raised in virtue and have not departed from it. Luther was probably in both of those categories. He never, at any point in his life, ever really committed deliberate sins of a grave nature... never knowingly turned his back on the Lord, or anything like that; and for this reason it was easy for Luther to think that trust in Christ guaranteed that good works would naturally, always flow out of the Christian. He was simply innocent and naive in this regard. The idea that someone could trust in Christ alone and yet engage in deliberate sin was foreign to his experience, something he could not understand. Many evangelicals fall into this camp as well, either because they have led a good Christian life since their conversion, and thus the good life seems to them guaranteed by it - or because they were raised well in the faith, and have never really committed grievous sins, and thus find it easy to believe that such things just don't happen when you truly believe.

There is plenty in Scripture which can be used to buttress such notions, i.e., "bad fruit cannot come from a good tree" and things to that effect. But bad actions can make a good tree bad, and a branch that does not bear fruit is severed and cast into fire. While there are some whose going out indicates they were never really within, the tongue can leak poison that destroys the body. Some seeds sprout up to new life, eagerly growing in the light of the Son, but then in times of trial make a shipwreck of their faith, and become filled with seven times more demons than they had before they escaped the defilements of the world. Like a dog they return to their vomit. Many of us believers have in the past done such things, and know from our own experience that all these passages are not just hypothetical warnings, but descriptions of what actually happens when we abandon repentance. Certainly, the gift of being born again - being made alive in the Spirit - is the key to the Christian life - even a hermeneutical key unlocking many texts on faith and works - and the necessary instrument through which good works flow. It is true that there is no good work or act of faith we can do to bring about this transformation, but the transformation does not reach the nuptial of justification within us, until it has brought about repentance within us, and the new life only resides within us so long as we abide in Him. None of this occurs apart from our cooperation with grace, and grace does not guarantee our cooperation. Being born-again truly works, and works abundantly, but it only works as long as we don't work against it. We can refuse to cooperate, we can abandon repentance; we can fall from grace, be cut off from the branch, and sever ourselves from Christ. Or we can strive to confirm our calling, to increase our righteousness and preserve our faith, and by doing so open the doors of Heaven wide, ensuring we make it through with ease.

Excursus 2
Imputation

Imputation Was Not Luther's Question

Before we explain, analyze, and critique the Protestant doctrine of Imputation, it's worth pointing out that Imputation was not the answer to Luther's reformation cry. While Reformed theologians sometimes claim the controversy boils down to this issue - that Imputation simply is the Gospel - the pressing concern for Luther was much more practical. He was not wrestling with speculative questions about ontology and formal causes, but rather, needed to know what he must do to be saved, and from whence he could derive certainty about the question. It was faith and works, and assurance, that so concerned Luther - and as I have tried to show in this book, the Catholic tradition has arrived at virtually identical solutions as those Luther proposed. For in the Lutheran and Reformed tradition - indeed in the broad Protestant tradition - in order to be saved you have to repent of sin and place your trust in God. That is all you have to do to be saved, and if you know you have done that, then you know you have been saved. And this is the same answer the Catholic Church offers. What must you do to be saved? Repent. And as long as you know you are repentant, you know you are saved.[60] The controversy over salvation has reached a point of mutual agreement. There is no practical difference. Luther's reformation cry, "what must I do to be saved?" has a common answer, and speculative questions surrounding formal causes, ontology, the hamartiology of concupiscence (i.e., all those things caught up in the doctrine of Imputation), etc., aren't relevant to that answer. Imputation simply was not Luther's question.

Now a Protestant may object, wanting to argue that the doctrine of Imputation, with its Simul Justus et Peccator, drives home a humility about deserving condemnation, forcing the Christian to trust in Christ alone, while the alternate Catholic doctrine of Infusion serves to bolster pride in self-righteousness, and foster, or at least enable, a certain form of self-trust. But this

---

[60] Calvinists and some Baptists will argue that once you repent, you can never lose your salvation, but these are only a minority of Protestants historically/statistically. Lutherans, most Anglicans, all Wesleyans, most Pentecostals, and many non-denominationals agree salvation is only maintained as long as you remain repentant and can be forfeit if you cease repenting/believing.

misunderstands the Catholic doctrine of Infusion. While grace infused into us makes us truly just, this does not come from us. It is, like with Imputation, an alien grace that is given to us, that comes to us from outside us (this is already explicit in the very etymology: Infusion, i.e., pouring in, from outside). While the Catholic in a state of grace may not *ontologically* deserve damnation in the present moment, they still have a track record of sin that deserves condemnation and are forbidden from trusting in themselves. The Catholic doctrine of Infusion does not allow self-trust because it heartedly affirms that not only our current standing in grace is due to God's mercy, but we could not persevere in it, indeed we would immediately fall from it, if God removed His mercy from us for but a single moment. Also, what is infused is grace and humility itself. To think infusion of grace enables self-trust is like saying infusion of malice engenders charity. It's an oxymoron. This may not get through to the lapsed and nominal Catholics that Ray Comfort meets on the street, but Catholics who actually participate in the faith and in the life of their parish are cognizant of their dependence on grace. The *Catechism* sets forth Therese of Lisieux's example on this point:

> 2011: The charity of Christ is the source in us of all our merits before God. Grace, by uniting us to Christ in active love, ensures the supernatural quality of our acts and consequently their merit before God and before men. The saints have always had a lively awareness that their merits were pure grace.
>
> > "After earth's exile, I hope to go and enjoy you in the fatherland, but I do not want to lay up merits for heaven. I want to work for your love alone.... In the evening of this life, I shall appear before you with empty hands, for I do not ask you, Lord, to count my works. All our justice is blemished in your eyes. I wish, then, to be clothed in your own justice and to receive from your love the eternal possession of yourself."[61]

When it comes to the Lutheran cry, "what must I do to be saved?", the Catholic and Protestant, if they are following the best of their traditions, both possess that twin disposition of assurance and humility, knowing themselves a sinner saved by grace, regardless of their perspective on the speculative ontological questions surrounding Imputation and Infusion.

---

[61] Therese of Lisieux, "Act of Offering" in *Story of a Soul*, trans. John Clarke (Washington, D.C.: ICS Publications, 1981), 277.

Indeed, those doctrines are more in the realm of anthropology than soteriology. Now this is not to dismiss the theological differences as irrelevant, but to place them in their proper context. The debate about Imputation is speculative, not practical. It's not pastoral, but technical - and technically, it boils down to the hamartiology of concupiscence in the regenerate.

Ontological or Legal?

If you listen to popular Catholic apologetics, it will often be said against Protestants: "salvation is not legal, it's ontological." Orthodox like to say this as well. And certainly, salvation is not a "legal fiction" (something Protestants would actually agree with). But salvation is legal. At least, both Scripture and the Catholic Church use legal metaphors and legal language to describe the event of justification (a word which in the Greek is often used in courtroom settings, as it seems to be used in Romans 2-4). Why did God become man? To satisfy the legal debt humanity incurred. At least, so says Anselm, Aquinas, and the entire Catholic tradition following them. Justification is not "not legal but ontological," it is a metaphor involving a legal declaration with a corresponding ontology.

Justification is ontological? This is weaponized against Protestants - but do Protestants disagree? Actually, no. What Protestants disagree with is the idea that our ontology is sufficient to serve as the formal cause of justification - but they are happy to affirm that the instrument of justification - our faith - is an ontological reality within us. Repentance, faith, regeneration... These are ontological changes within us. And Protestants agree they are involved with, and are necessary components of, justification. A person cannot be justified apart from these ontological changes. A person is infused with sanctifying grace and charity? The language might not be Protestant, but the substance is. *"God pours forth His love into our hearts through the Holy Spirit"* (Rom. 5:5). Which Protestant denies that this infusion of love and ontological change occurs when God justifies us?

The debate between Catholic Infusion and Protestant Imputation is not about whether justification is legal or ontological. Both affirm that both occur. The difference is precisely, and only, with regard to the hamartiology of the concupiscence that remains in the regenerate. The Protestant deems those inclinations to be mortal sins deserving of Hell in and of themselves, and thus finds a need for an extrinsic imputation. The Catholic sees that these inclinations, insofar as they are in the regenerate, are unwilled by the Christian, and are struggled against, and despised by us, and therefore says along with

Paul, *"It is no longer I who do them"* *(Rom. 7)*. We are not culpable for them. And because the concupiscence which remains in the regenerate is not something we are culpable for, the Catholic sees no need for an additional imputation.

Infused Righteousness

It can sometimes get lost in the confusion of the debates, but it is worth pointing out that infused righteousness is not a doctrine unique to Catholicism. Every Protestant affirms the existence of infused righteousness within the Christian. In fact, Protestants would not allow for justification apart from it. For faith, repentance, regeneration… whether taken individually, or all together, are all examples of infused righteousness. Every virtue, every disposition towards the good, everything inside us that orients us towards God, all of these are only possible by grace, only possible when God infuses them into us, and they are all examples of righteousness. The debate between Catholics and Protestants therefore is not about whether justification involves infused righteousness. Protestants affirm that infused righteousness is involved. The question is whether infused righteousness relates only to the instrumental cause of justification (as Protestants would claim), or whether it is sufficient to serve as the formal cause (as the Catholic Church teaches).

Romans 7 and the Hamartiology of Concupiscence

A key text, or at least, a debated text, for thinking about sin in the Christian life, is Romans 7. In that chapter Paul describes a struggle with indwelling sin and a frustration with not experiencing victory over it. Lutherans tend to think their doctrine of Simul Justus et Peccator finds its theological grounding there. Catholic commentators sometimes pushback, along with a growing number of Protestant scholars, arguing that the experience described by Paul in Rom. 7 is not that of the Christian because in the very next chapter Paul says that Christians experience victory over sin. This interpretation makes sense, of course, since Ch. 7 indicates a struggle and Ch. 8 indicates a victory. But Catholics do not need to take this approach, as if the experience of struggle with sin cannot be understood as describing the Christian life which is also victorious over it. Indeed, Luther's understanding of this was simply a repetition of what Augustine had written some thousand years before he was born.

If we are going to interpret Romans 7 in terms of the Christian experience, we need to do so in a way that harmonizes with the following chapter. How can the Christian both struggle with sin and have victory over it at the same time? Augustine offers a more than plausible approach. While Christians do experience the gradually increasing victory over sin described in chapter 8, the internal inclinations of concupiscence remain within them, warring against the desires of the Spirit, and are only slowly put to death over time. Therefore, the struggle with indwelling sin described in chapter 7 is always a reality within the Christian - there is never a time on this side of glory that we do not struggle with temptations, internal battles, etc. But as we walk by the Spirit, we slowly put those desires to death, and gradually experience more and more freedom from them, as described in chapter 8. Important for this approach is that the person described in chapter 7 does not embrace the temptations, but rather hates them and struggles against them, and for this reason can truly say *"it is no longer I who do these things, but sin that dwells in me" (v. 20)*. The person who deliberately consents to the inclination and commits the suggested sin cannot say such a thing. Only the person who remains repentant in the midst of sinful inclinations, struggles against them and puts them to death by walking in the Spirit, experiences both Romans 7 and 8 at the same time. This is the interpretation that Augustine offered.

Luther agreed with Augustine about this interpretation. From his *Commentary on Romans*:

> In this way, then, you should understand chapter 7, where St. Paul portrays himself as still a sinner, while in chapter 8 he says that, because of the incomplete gifts and because of the Spirit, there is nothing damnable in those who are in Christ. Because our flesh has not been killed, we are still sinners, but because we believe in Christ and have the beginnings of the Spirit, God so shows us his favor and mercy, that he neither notices nor judges such sins. Rather he deals with us according to our belief in Christ until sin is killed... ...St. Paul takes up the special work of faith, the struggle which the spirit wages against the flesh to kill off those sins and desires that remain after a person has been made just. He teaches us that faith doesn't so free us from sin that we can be idle, lazy and self-assured, as though there were no more sin in us. Sin is there, but, because of faith that struggles against it, God does not reckon sin as deserving damnation.

Several things are important about this quote from Luther. The primary thing to notice, however, is what he says about our culpability or guilt for the inclinations we struggle against. God *"neither notices nor judges such sins"* and *"sin is there, but, because of faith that struggles against it, God does not reckon sin as deserving damnation."* By saying these things Luther has almost conceded the Catholic position. The reason why the regenerate does not need an imputation is because the inclinations to sin that remain within them are not things they are culpable for. Because they do not will them, nor consent to them, but hate them and struggle against them, there is no guilt incurred on behalf of them.

Now Luther would assuredly say that while God in His grace does not reckon the inclinations as sin, that nevertheless God would, apart from grace, if judging in strict justice, deem them as deserving Hell - this is why Luther believed an imputation was necessary. But elsewhere in the same work Luther defines sin in the following way:

> Sin in the Scriptures means not only external works of the body but also all those movements within us which bestir themselves and move us to do the external works, namely, the depth of the heart with all its powers. Therefore the word "do" should refer to a person's completely falling into sin. No external work of sin happens, after all, unless a person commit himself to it completely, body and soul. In particular, the Scriptures see into the heart, to the root and main source of all sin: unbelief in the depth of the heart.

Notice that while Luther identifies sin with all the things within us that move us to sin, he also wants to emphasize that no one "does" sin unless they do it themselves, i.e., unless they actually commit themselves to it. Luther may not have followed this line of thinking all the way to its logical conclusion, but that is the line of thinking the Church bases its teaching on. Certainly, sin is found in the depths of the heart, but it is not something we are culpable for unless we actually do it ourselves. If we can honestly say, along with Paul, *"it is no longer I who do it, but sin that dwells in me"*, then we are not guilty of it, even in strict justice (for God knows that we aren't the one doing it), for we did not do it, and are not responsible for it. Once this has been accepted, an extrinsic imputation becomes superfluous. Regeneration has already made the person righteous. Their sins have already been covered and washed.

The Alien Righteousness of Abraham's Faith

For He made Him who knew no sin to be sin for us, that we might become the righteousness of God in Him. (2 Cor. 5:21)

I have lost all things. I consider them rubbish, that I may gain Christ and be found in Him, not having my own righteousness from the law, but that which is through faith in Christ, the righteousness from God on the basis of faith. (Phil. 3:8-9)

To the one who does not work but trusts God who justifies the ungodly, their faith is credited as righteousness. (Rom. 4:5)

These three passages of Scripture teach that righteousness does not come from ourselves. We receive righteousness from outside of ourselves, because of Christ, despite our own unrighteousness. If God only justified the righteous, He would justify no one: "*For none are righteous - no, not one*" *(Rom. 3:10)*. But to the one who does not work, but trusts in the God who justifies the unjust? Their faith is credited as righteousness. God comes to us in His grace, finds us in our sin and unbelief, and works within us to convert us, to move us to repentance, and impart His righteousness to us. This means the righteousness is alien: it does not come from within, but from without. God condescends to sinners, not the other way around. This is true with Infusion, of course. The very word is explicit in that regard. God "infuses" grace and righteousness into us, from outside of us. It does not sprout from within. The Christian is not justified because they are just within, but the inverse: they become just within because God justifies them. Cardinal Avery Dulles pointed this out some time ago,

> It would be wrong to imagine that we are pronounced righteous because we are inherently such. Rather the reverse: any inherent righteousness of ours is consequent upon God's gracious, creative sentence of pardon.[62]

Catholic scholar Fr. Joseph Fitzmyer says the same (righteousness is alien):

> Paul insists on the utter gratuity of this justification, because "all alike have sinned and fall short of the glory of God" (3:23). Consequently, this uprightness does not belong to human beings (10:3), and it is not something that they have produced or merited; it is an alien uprightness, one belonging

---

[62] Dulles, 258.

rightly to another (to Christ) and attributed to them because of what that other has done for them. So Paul understands God "justifying the godless" (4:5) or "crediting uprightness" to human beings quite "apart from deeds.[63]

Does this not constitute an endorsement of the Protestant doctrine of imputation and a rejection of the Catholic doctrine of infusion? Not hardly. As we have been saying, inherent righteousness exists in us consequent to God's gracious justifying declaration on our behalf. It is important to emphasize that God is not justifying us because we are inherently just. God does not justify the inherently just. He justifies the inherently unjust, and in doing so, makes them inherently just. Unfortunately, in popular debates many Catholics make it seem otherwise, especially with the accusations of nominalism against Protestants, in, "God cannot declare someone just if they are not actually just." But this betrays the fact that no one can be just unless God first declares them to be. And it is precisely (and only), the unjust, whom God takes, and declares, and makes just.

But there is some tension here that needs to be unraveled and explained. The Catholic teaching is that intrinsic righteousness is the formal cause of justification. How can we reconcile the priority of God's declaration, and the inability for justification to be real within the individual unless they are just themselves? There is an idea in Reformed theology that helps us here, for they say, "regeneration precedes faith," but that this is not a priority in time. The priority is understood to be logical rather than temporal. The idea is that regeneration produces faith, logically, but that the two come to exist simultaneously. Whether right or wrong about regeneration and faith, the Reformed distinction between logical priority and temporal succession is valuable for understanding the Catholic teaching of justification and infusion. God's declaration of our justification comes first - our internal justice cannot exist unless the declaration precedes it and causes it. But this is not a succession in time. It is a logical priority, God's declaration that we are justified immediately causes, simultaneously, our being made just internally.

But another thing is important here. When we speak of God justifying the unjust, we are speaking in terms of metaphor. It is not as if God actually declares the words "This man is justified", and the sound of His voice carries sanctifying grace into the soul, making His verbal declaration real within us. We can speak this way about what happens, but it's only a way of speaking about it. And it is a particularly New Covenant way of speaking. The Old Testament

---

[63] Fitzmyer, *Commentary on Romans*, 118.

text used by Paul as his precedent for justification comes from Genesis 15:6, where we are told that *"Abraham believed God, and this was credited to him as righteousness."* In Christian theology we talk about God taking the sinner, converting them, and justifying them, i.e., declaring them just. And that's a valid application and development of this passage in Genesis. Paul is using Abraham to bolster his own justification-in-the-court-of-law metaphor; and certainly, it is true that God came to Abraham, before Abraham ever believed, and worked His grace into Abraham, converting and declaring Abraham justified. All very true. But the passage in Genesis was not saying exactly that. What Genesis says is that God looked upon Abraham's faith, and God deemed Abraham's action of believing the promise to be a righteous action. "Abraham believed God, and this was credited to him as righteousness." This is an ethical evaluation of faith. When a human sinner, in a world God has allowed to be filled with death and suffering, nevertheless looks up to the Heavens, and says, "God is good, God is righteous, I trust in Him" - that's the only kind of righteousness that God is interested in, or at least, the necessary root and beginning of all such righteousness. Our works are utterly useless in His eyes - He has no need for them. We can give nothing to Him. He can do everything He wants to do, all on His own. What He needs from us is simply faith. God likes faith. He accounts it, considers it, judges it to be righteousness.

This is relevant for Imputation because when God justifies Abraham, God is not imputing an extrinsic righteousness to Abraham's account. Rather, God is making an ethical evaluation of Abraham's faith. Abraham's faith is accounted, it's judged, it's determined to be righteous. The decision to trust God, to believe God, was righteousness in God's eyes. The righteousness within Abraham - his faith - of course came to him, from outside him, when he was still an unrighteous sinner. And yet, the righteousness was now within him. God had worked it into him, converted him, worked faith into him, worked the righteousness of faith into him. There is a dialectic here, to be sure. Abraham was a sinner, but God counted his faith as righteousness. How can this be? Think of this question: is it good or wicked for a sinner to admit their guilt? Of course, it is good and righteous to admit your guilt. Jerome comments on this dialectic in *Against the Pelagians*:

> We are then righteous when we confess that we are sinners, and our righteousness depends not upon our own merits, but on the mercy of God, as the Holy Scripture says, "The righteous man accuses himself when he begins to speak," and elsewhere, "Tell your sins that you may be justified," and "God has shut up all under sin, that He may have mercy upon

all." And the highest righteousness of man is this — whatever virtue he may be able to acquire, not to think it his own, but the gift of God.

You are guilty, but by admitting your guilt you do what is righteous. You become righteous, at least in this regard. The fact that confession of guilt and faith in God come out as righteous actions when their ethical qualities are evaluated does not necessarily prove the doctrine of Imputation wrong. The Protestant would of course admit that repentance, conversion, faith, etc., are all ethically good actions. But given that Abraham's justification, in Genesis, was a justification precisely in terms of this sort of ethical evaluation, the argument against justification as an extrinsic imputation is strengthened considerably. Imputation was not, at least, what was going on with Abraham in Genesis 15:6. Abraham's justification was an ethical evaluation of his disposition, not an extrinsic imputation.

Cause and Formal Cause

The question the Protestant doctrine of Imputation seeks to answer is not a practical question, like Luther's cry, "how can I, a sinner, find mercy from a holy God?" Luther's question was motivated by concerns about *instrumentality* - what must I do to *receive* salvation? But Imputation doesn't address the instrument of justification; it attempts to describe the formal cause of it. Here there may be some confusion about different types of causes. The Catholic Church distinguishes between four causes of new covenant justification: the instrumental cause, the formal cause, the meritorious cause, and the final cause. "Faith alone causes salvation," but in what sense? Faith is an *instrumental* cause, for it is *through* faith that grace is received. "By Christ alone we are justified," but in what way? His death on the cross *merited* for us the grace of salvation. "For God's glory we are saved." Yes, but in what manner? In of that, the final purpose of salvation, the ultimate reason why we are saved at all, is to behold and enjoy the glory of God forever. God's glory is thus the *final cause* of our justification. So far, with regard to the instrumental, meritorious, and final causes of our justification, Catholics and Protestants are in agreement. It is the question of the formal cause that brings Imputation and Infusion to center stage.

In Protestant teaching the formal cause of justification is the personal righteousness of Christ, external to the believer, legally imputed to their account, such that although they remain internally unrighteous before God, they have this external imputation of Christ's righteousness covering them, and the ledger of God's judgment considers them just even though they are intrinsically unjust. This is the *Simul Justus et Peccator* - simultaneously just and sinner - of Protestant teaching which grounds the doctrine of Imputation. The Christian is said to be intrinsically unrighteous and sinful before God, even after they have been regenerated and justified, such that if God in strict justice were to judge the ontology of their soul, it would be found deserving of Hell. This is because in the Protestant's view, love of God and regeneration do not make a person actually righteous. The unwilled inclinations towards sin which remain in us are considered objective mortal sins that we remain guilty of, and because of this we need an external righteousness outside of ourselves - the righteousness of Christ - to be legally imputed, or accounted, to our ledger, so that God can consider us righteous.

In Catholicism it is understood that though a certain inclination to sin remains in the believer after they are justified, because the inclination (concupiscence) is unwilled by the believer, it is therefore *"no longer I who do it, but sin living in me" (Rom. 7:17)*. Because it is not something the believer is doing, but is rather something they struggle against, it is not something that they are culpable of. It does not make them guilty. And since in regeneration and justification God has infused supernatural love for Christ into our hearts, they have by that very infusion become internally, "formally," righteous. The formal cause of our justification - the "form" of being in a right relationship with God - is the simple fact that we love Him. And God loves us. Salvation is "formed" by that relationship. Just like in human relationships, where a person desires and loves another, but the two do not have a relationship until the other returns that love, but the moment they do, the love they have for the other person is the entirely sufficient basis for their relationship. So too with us and God. He already loves each and every one of us. But we do not love Him, and thus do not have a relationship with Him. But once He infuses love for Himself into our souls, then the fact we love Him becomes the basis for our relationship - the formal cause of it.

Relationship, Not Religion

Among evangelicals there is a popular slogan: Christianity is a relationship, not a religion. The slogan is unpopular outside the non-denominational world, primarily because Christianity is a religion. But the semantic range of the word now includes a certain kind of legalism that focuses on external rituals and neglects sincerity of heart. For this reason, the phrase ("not a religion") is understandable... Christianity is certainly not supposed to be that sort of religion. Another reason some dislike the slogan is because they think it overly sentimental and squishy. I would nudge such people with a quote from Augustine, "*So there you are, that's really what welcoming Jesus means, welcoming him into your heart*" (Sermon 174). The heart of the Christian faith really is condensable into something like the sinner's prayer and an altar call. We are all, each one of us, no matter how far along in the Christian life we may be, in the same place as the Thief on the Cross. To put it another way: the ground is level at the foot of the Cross. The kingdom is only open to those who become like little children, and to look down on a relationship with the Lord, giving your heart to Him, praying the sinner's prayer at the altar, is to flirt dangerously with a pharisaical legalism that can be downright fatal to the spiritual life. But now that I have preached a little, let's get back to the original topic.

Interestingly, this principle - that salvation is a relationship with God - is actually the reason why Protestant Imputation is misguided. Salvation depends on, and consists in, a relationship with God. And what "forms" the basis of a relationship? Love. Now God loves everyone, but not everyone loves God, and so not everyone is in relationship with Him. But once a person has received from God an infusion into their hearts of supernatural love for Him, then this by itself forms the basis of their justification and their salvation. There is no need for an extrinsic imputation to establish a salvific relationship, the person is already supernaturally in love with God. Love is the basis and form of every relationship, and our relationship with God is no different. Cardinal Cajetan articulated this back in 1532 in his letter to Pope Clement VII. The letter is entitled "On faith and works." See his explanation of the role of love in justification below:

> Charity is this friendship between man and God, being both man's love of friendship toward God and God's toward man. "God is love, and he who abides in love abides in God, and God in him." We read in the same epistle, "We love God, because he first loved us." Since friendship consists in mutual love, the forgiveness of sins takes place essentially through charity. Hence what we call the righteousness of faith is identical with charity.

Justification defined in terms of love for God represents the heart of the Catholic critique of Protestant imputation. Luther and those following him wanted to exclude love from the basis of justification (though not from its fruits), and this is understandable given the impossibility of love prior to justification. But the Catholic teaching says that justification comes to undeserving sinners precisely in the form of love. It is not that a person needs to first love God in order to then be justified. Rather, the guilty sinner with no love or works whatsoever, is moved by grace to repent and turn towards God, and God runs to the prodigal, embracing them, restoring the relationship by infusing love into their heart. That is how God justified us, and this forms the basis of the salvific relationship. Love.

In addition to love there is no need for an imputation, especially because whatever struggles with sin that remain, are unwilled and despised by the Christian. The Christian hates the temptations, and struggles against them. They do not represent the Christian's heart, which has been regenerated and filled with supernatural love for God. At that point, the Christian can say about any remaining inclinations towards sin, *"it is no longer I who do it" (Rom 7:17)*, and therefore is not culpable for them. The love for God infused into their heart has formed the basis of a saving relationship with Him. In the words of the Council of Trent, contra Protestant Imputation, love for God - a personal relationship with Jesus - is the formal cause and basis of our salvation. That is what Christianity is: a relationship, not a religion. To require anything in addition to love for God, whether imputation, or any external ritual, or even anything internal - anything at all - as if sincere love for God was not enough, is indeed the worst form of legalism, the worst form of religion.

Pastoral Concerns

Protestants push back against this doctrine of Infusion with vigor. The idea we can stand before God on the basis of our own interior righteousness seems Pelagian and blasphemous. We are all sinners; how can we stand before God on the basis of our own righteousness? But God doesn't justify the righteous, but the unrighteous: *"to the one who does not work but trusts in Him who justifies the ungodly, his faith is credited for righteousness."* And the Protestant has a point. It would be wrong to think that God only justifies those who are just. For that would be impossible. But the Catholic teaching does not conceive of God justifying the just. Rather, when God takes an unrighteous person and justifies them, He infuses love into them, and in so doing, makes the unjust just. Cardinal Avery Dulles wrote,

> It would be wrong to imagine that we are pronounced righteous because we are inherently such. Rather the reverse:

any inherent righteousness of ours is consequent upon God's gracious, creative sentence of pardon.[64]

What does Scripture say? There are many statements which indicate that righteousness comes from outside of us, that it is a gift of grace given to unrighteous people on the basis of Christ's righteousness and not their own. But Catholics agree with all this. Righteousness is a gift given to us, from outside of us, from God, on the basis of the Cross, despite our sins. And yet, in the texts Protestants find the strongest evidence for Imputation, nowhere is the doctrine of an extrinsic imputation actually explicitly taught. *"Christ became sin so that we might become the righteousness of God."* Note that this doesn't say Christ became sin so that we would be considered righteousness, but that so we would "become" righteous. How about: *"Not having a righteousness of my own that comes from the law, but that which comes through faith in Christ, the righteousness from God that depends on faith."* Remember, the Catholic doctrine of infused righteousness is explicitly defined in terms of infusion, i.e., it comes from outside of us, is infused into us, by God. It is not our own, not something we generated or created. It is infused into us despite our unrighteousness. It makes us righteous, but this is not a righteousness we can call "our own" any more than the Protestant can call their faith in God "their own," for all of these gifts indwell the Christian, but none of them are of our own making.

While I think Imputation is erroneous, it is easy to understand the pastoral concerns a Protestant might have with the Catholic view. Pastorally, an "inherent righteousness" could present several problems. Despair: "how could I ever be saved on the basis of my own righteousness, given I know my internal struggles with sin and how unrighteous I am?" Pride: "I am so holy; I can stand before God on my own interior sanctity. I have nothing truly sinful within me." Clearly, if the Catholic doctrine is not preached correctly, it could be fatal. The Protestant solution is the motto, "Simul Justus et Peccator." The Protestant tells themself that although they are a damnable sinner, they have received the gift of Christ's righteousness. "I am beloved by Christ, indwelt by the Spirit, walking the path of sanctification, and yet I am a sinner, imperfect, with my own failings and struggles." We must admit this disposition is a pleasing one, confidence in God's mercy in the admission of personal guilt, humility, and joy together. But the Catholic, even the justified Catholic, is taught to pray in every Mass: "through my fault, my most grievous fault, I have greatly sinned, in my thoughts, in my words, in what I have done and failed to do." We pray every day in the Lord's prayer, asking God to "forgive us our

---

[64] Dulles, 258.

sins." Though in this present moment I may not be currently culpable of mortal sin, the only possible reason is that God in His mercy has graciously forgiven me in virtue of Christ's death. Even in grace, we constantly struggle with concupiscence, desires for sins, and if we are not committing mortal sins, we are still committing venial sins daily. Therefore, a good and true Catholic version of Simul Justus et Peccator can be readily adopted, remembering that any righteousness inherent in us is due solely to the grace of God and not to anything we did or could do, and remembering the words of our Lord, *"When you have done all that I command you, say, 'We have done what we ought, we are unworthy servants" (Luke 17:10).* We go forward to receive Jesus, confessing "Lord, I am unworthy that you should enter under my roof," and with confidence praying "but only say the word and my soul shall be healed." And then we receive, and know we have received, Him – body, blood, soul and divinity.

"The Justice of God"

At the beginning of this story, we read about Luther's wrestling with Paul's phrase "the justice of God." He read in the Book of Romans that the Gospel revealed the 'justice,' or 'righteousness' of God. Luther had been frightened by this phrase because he thought that the Gospel revealed that God was a just and righteous judge who would punish the guilty. When he discovered that what the Gospel actually reveals is the promise of justification for the unjust, Luther felt as if he was born again. The comfort and relief this brought him was life-changing, and ultimately, history-changing as well. While we can take Luther's word for it that he had been taught by Catholics an incorrect understanding of "the justice of God," we can also agree with Luther about the correct meaning of the phrase. The Church has always, though perhaps not always in all of her members (as Luther claims), understood the phrase in terms of God's justification of sinners. Augustine articulated that contrast long before Luther was born - and Catholics had of course read Augustine. In *Spirit and Letter,* he wrote the following:

> But now the righteousness of God, says he, without the law is manifested... Now this righteousness they are ignorant of, who wish to establish one of their own; they will not submit themselves to it... the righteousness of God - But the righteousness of God by faith of Jesus Christ, that is by the faith wherewith one believes in Christ, for just as there is not meant the faith with which Christ Himself believes, so also there is not meant the righteousness whereby God is Himself

righteous. Both no doubt are ours, but yet they are called God's, and Christ's, because it is by their bounty that these gifts are bestowed upon us.

And the Council of Trent repeats this same understanding of the righteousness of God, emphasizing that it only comes to man on the basis of Christ's merits; and that it is that particular justice whereby God justifies sinners:

> The meritorious cause is His most beloved only-begotten, our Lord Jesus Christ, who, when we were enemies, for the exceeding charity wherewith he loved us, merited Justification for us by His most holy Passion on the wood of the cross, and made satisfaction for us unto God the Father... the alone formal cause is the justice of God, not that whereby He Himself is just, but that whereby He maketh us just.

This righteousness comes to us from outside of us, because of Christ, and it is Christ's grace that fills us and makes us righteous. Discussing this at the Council of Trent, Archbishop Bartolomeo Carranza de Miranda, O.P., offered the following explanation:

> The air is illuminated by the sun, yet it is not formally lit by the light of the sun. So thus we are justified by Christ effectively and meritoriously, but we are not just formally by the justice which is in Christ, but by that which is in us, in which we have partaken from Christ and which depends on Christ constantly.

The righteousness of God, the justification we receive from Him, comes to us despite our guilt, despite our own unrighteousness. It was won for us on the Cross by the merits of Christ. It is God's way of mercifully justifying sinners. On these points the Catholic Church is in agreement with Luther.